AFTER THE "SPECULATIVE TURN"

BEFORE YOU START TO READ THIS BOOK, take this moment to think about making a donation to punctum books, an independent non-profit press,

@ https://punctumbooks.com/support/

If you're reading the e-book, you can click on the image below to go directly to our donations site. Any amount, no matter the size, is appreciated and will help us to keep our ship of fools afloat. Contributions from dedicated readers will also help us to keep our commons open and to cultivate new work that can't find a welcoming port elsewhere. Our adventure is not possible without your support.
Vive la open-access.

Fig. 1. Hieronymus Bosch, *Ship of Fools* (1490–1500)

First published in 2016 by punctum books, Earth, Milky Way.
https://punctumbooks.com

ISBN-13: 978-0-9982375-3-4
ISBN-10: 0-9982375-3-1
Library of Congress Cataloging Data is available from the Library of Congress

Book design: Vincent W.J. van Gerven Oei

AFTER THE "SPECULATIVE TURN"
Realism, Philosophy,
and Feminism

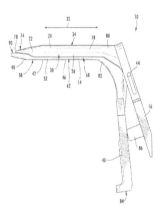

Edited by Katerina Kolozova and Eileen A. Joy

Contents

Preface: After the "Speculative Turn"

Katerina Kolozova

Recent forms of realism in continental philosophy, habitually subsumed under the (not always coherent) category of "speculative realism," have provided grounds for the much needed critique of social-constructivist approaches in gender theory and of the authority with which various forms of post-structuralist critique have dominated feminist theory for decades.[1] But the interest in realism and in the possibility of a universalism that would still remain post-metaphysical displayed in most of the feminist (speculative) realist or (new) materialist writings I have

---

1   For an important critique of the idea that newer work in feminist realisms and "new materialisms" moves against the grain of an earlier feminist scholarship not concerned enough with matter and matter-ing, see Sara Ahmed, "Some Preliminary Remarks on the Founding Gestures of the 'New Materialism'," *European Journal of Women's Studies* 15, no. 1 (2008): 23–39, where she writes that "the very claim that matter is missing can actually work to reify matter as if it could be an object that is absent or present. By turning matter into an object or theoretical category, in this way, the new materialism reintroduces the binarism between materiality and culture that much work in science studies has helped to challenge" (35). Ahmed's intervention into work on newer feminist materialisms is important to take into account here, while also recognizing, as Ahmed herself does, that, "[g]iven the feminist concern with understanding how gender and sexuality are reproduced in time and space, a key emphasis [in feminist critique] has been placed on language, culture, the symbolic, labour, discourse and ideology. This is because feminism needs a theory of social reproduction; of how particular forms become norms over time" (33).

read so far has been purely epistemological. There is no political motivation in those writings and they have most certainly not been directed against cultural theory per se vis-à-vis its domination over questions of gender, sexual difference and other forms of social philosophy discourse. In 2014 Iris van der Tuin and Peta Hinton wrote that,

> as well as being timely in its inquiry, the need to mark out a feminist politics of/within new materialism is also, and clearly, an 'untimely' project. And if we shift this focus on time to consider the contemporaneity of new materialist scholarship and its ethico-political developments, the need to address its feminist temperament (as well as the shapes that feminism assumes) becomes increasingly clear. A review of the field will show that, to date, most compendiums on new materialism seem more broadly oriented or implicitly feminist in their direction, without necessarily picking up with what feminist new materialism 'looks like' as a focus of inquiry. This is another way of saying that the question of the political in the context of new materialism has been asked in such a way that, while new materialist ways of conceptualizing positive difference/differing have been devised […] the question of the political has not yet been answered with specific regard to feminist politics.[2]

The interest in new forms of realism is thus still largely abstract, essentially epistemological and sparked by the relativism of "postmodern theory" as a philosophical impasse to be overcome, rather than motivated by the political implications of post-structuralist critique's undisputed authority in most humanities departments worldwide. I would argue, however, that new forms of realist materialism could have significant political ramifications that should be more owned by feminist scholars as a way to create new possibilities for an internationalist feminist political language and action that would be geographically,

2   Peta Hinton and Iris van der Tuin, "Preface," *Women: A Cultural Review* 25, no. 1, special issue on "Feminist Matters: The Politics of New Materialism" (2014): 1–8, at 4.

economically and in terms of nation-state politics, as varied and as multi-centered as possible. Such a new universalism must emerge at the economic and academic margins and provide the grounds for uncompromising comradeship worldwide. The universe it will establish is one in which power will be measured in materialist or realist terms and its chief categories will be also the most robust ones: economy and the power of the nation-state as the main means of women's subjugation. Identity, culture, sexuality, and all other major "real abstractions" (Marx) will be as relevant in such a worldview as any other issue that is plaguing women, but they will not be the norm that hierarchically structures all of our priorities.

At this early point in the Preface, I must underscore that none of what is stated above, in my imaginary new world of feminist universalism, is either said or implied by the authors represented in the book at hand. What unites them in a single book, following the initial conceptualization of this project by myself and its former editors Michael O'Rourke and Ben Woodard, is the significance of their feminist contributions to realist thought and to the building of possibilities for new universalisms regardless of their affiliation with "speculative realism," "object oriented ontology," or other "new materialisms" as such. "New" here refers to non-reactionary, non-revisionist, and non-reformist stances with regard to any history of philosophy predating structuralism, a stance committed to re-inventing the possibility of a universal language for a feminist international movement of the twenty-first century.

Although there is no unequivocal meaning behind the term "speculative realism," the reference remains in the title. It does so because the name itself refers to a certain critical event in the intellectual history of the beginning of the twenty-first century.[3]

3   Many sources could be cited, but a good touchstone vis-a-vis our own volume with regard to the recent advent of "speculative realism" would be Levi Bryant, Nick Srnicek, and Graham Harman (eds.), *The Speculative Turn: Continental Materialism and Realism* (Melbourne: re.press, 2011), a volume which featured only one woman (Isabelle Stengers) among its twenty-one contributors.

It is an event that self-constitutes the need for a "realist turn" that will fundamentally reinvent the ideas of the real, reality, and realism as inherited from the Western philosophical tradition. The theory, as well as the artistic and political practice, inspired by "speculative realism" display the need for a radical break with most of this philosophical tradition and declare the poststructuralist legacy fundamentally indebted to (if not a direct continuation of) the classical philosophical traditions, and more specifically to the post-Kantian one. In other words, the attempts toward the creation of new realisms that go under the common name of "speculative realism" may have failed partly or fully, but what is important is that, in all of their heterogeneity, they constitute a radical break with the canonical philosophical traditions. "Speculative realism" has been especially marked by considerations of scientific practice. Its project is, however, fundamentally different from that of the philosophy of science or science of philosophy. In spite of the heterogeneity of the different strands constituting it, "speculative realism" is defined by a radical break with any form of philosophical spontaneity. The latter is a term often used by Laruelle in his critique of the principle of philosophical sufficiency: philosophy always already and by definition establishes a relation of amphibology with the real, a relation of thought and the real co-creating one another whereby the former determines the latter. The new forms of realism attempt to produce theory that acknowledges the asymmetry between thought and the real while affirming that the determination in the last instance of any form of truth must be an instance of the real. It is precisely this stance they have in common with scientific practice.

Feminist philosophy, moving away from philosophical spontaneity, was founded upon several grounding gestures that have put into question philosophy's pretension of placing itself beyond sociality and beyond patriarchal ideology in order to posit itself as superior to other forms of intellectual production based on its "non-contingent" constitution. Luce Irigaray has postulated that speculation is at the heart of Western rationality and that it is nothing more than an extension of the patriarchal Symbolic and the language dictated by it. The "object" of philosophical study is but a reflection of the auto-referential subject. Further, also according to Irigaray, the philosophical subject of the great Western tradition of rational(ist) thought has legislated for itself the position of highest authority on the matters of truth and real/ity. Although other feminist philosophers have not used the same terminology nor have proposed the same or similar analysis, many feminist scholars have shared the claim that the subject/object binary is informed by patriarchal ideology and that philosophy has never been ideologically innocent or beyond the Symbolic and its language. In spite of the numerous and significant differences, such positions have been advocated by Donna Haraway, Judith Butler, Rosi Braidotti, and many others. In other words, for the feminism of the late twentieth century and the beginning of the twenty-first century, the claim that philosophy is essentially patriarchal and masculinist has extended beyond the post-Kantian epistemic condition and its prevalence in the era. The claim is not only that knowledge is "subjective," but also that the access to the real, to the "out-there," is a priori barred. It is also a claim that the transcendental, or the minimum structure of rationality and language, is fundamentally gendered. The subject of the speculative mind mirrors the object and posits it as the real instead of the real (referring to the issue of amphibology explained above). Hysterical utterings, on the other hand, depart from the real or the physical (Irigaray). Biological difference becomes the fundament of a new language that moves away from abstract postulations detached from the physicality as essentially masculinist (Braidotti). The practice of grief becomes the material for a new political language (Butler). Sexual difference as materiality understood in Freudian terms precedes the social (Copjec). In short, the provocations of "speculative turn" philosophers (generally, all men) to post-Kantianism were already preceded by feminist philosophy.

Therefore, after the "speculative turn," whose interests seem (if unconsciously) to have converged with those of feminist philosophy, the classical philosophical traditions remain relevant for feminist philosophy. The possibility that has been open for feminism since 2006 is to pursue its radical critique of Western philosophy without the burden of maintaining fidelity to the linguistic turn, to the dogma of postmodernism and poststructrualism and their ostracisms of the real and realisms as reactionary. It has served as an occasion to reclaim feminist forms of realism without revisionism but rather as its (realism's) reinventions founded on the remnants of the history of the Western philosophical tradition.

I claim that Foucault is not reducible to poststructuralism, and that poststructuralism is certainly not about social constructivism. I also claim that structuralism remains relevant for feminism, as do deconstruction and the ideas of Deleuze, but that they invite different languages and methodological possibilities if situated critically with regard to the event of the so called "speculative turn." Regardless of whether she adheres to the strand of thought that has labeled itself "speculative realism" or not, each author that has contributed to this collection has demonstrated that the terrain of "postmodernity" has been fundamentally destabilized in the beginning of the twenty-first century.

This collection brings to the fore some of the feminist debates prompted by the so-called "speculative turn" and also some that have remained untouched by it, but ultimately this volume demonstrates that feminism has moved away from the "postmodern condition" and its epistemologies. It also demonstrates that there has never been a niche of "speculative realist feminism." But it also problematizes the designation of "speculative realism" itself and of any pretension to assign to it an unequivocal meaning.

Some of the essays featured here tackle object-oriented ontology while providing a feminist critical challenge to its paradigms, while others refer to some extent to non-philosophy or to new materialism and new realism without necessarily performing their "feminist version." The majority, however, do not refer to any of the particular currents of "speculative realism." Instead, they constitute a critical theory sui generis that invokes the necessity of foregrounding new forms of realism for a "feminism beyond gender as culture." We have purposefully invited essays from intellectual milieus outside the Anglo-Saxon academic center, bringing together authors from Serbia, Slovenia, France, the UK, and Canada. In this way we are prefiguring one form of strategic mobilization for a feminist internationalism that will replace gestures of generosity and paternalism consisting of "cultural inclusion." The internationalism we propose will ultimately be in need of a reinvented feminist universalism that will hopefully be grounded in new forms of realism and (Marxist) materialism for feminist theory and political practice.

In the end, I would like to thank Michel O'Rourke for the initiative to edit a book such as this one, and for providing the blueprint for its concept with his seminal article "Girls Welcome!!!" which we have republished in this volume. Many thanks to Ben Woodard and Eileen Joy for contributing to the editing process, and to Vincent van Gerven Oei for the typesetting and wonderful cover.

Philosophy, Sexism, Emotion, Rationalism

Nina Power

Something important is happening within and to Philosophy.[1] It is something that has happened a thousand times over, yet every time it repeats it happens as if for the first time. The difficulty is making this event stick. What is this event? The event of the disruption of Philosophy by its own outside, the outside that it pretends it does not have. Philosophy, by virtue of being the most universal subject, the most generic art, cannot imagine that there is something which it cannot capture or has not *always already* captured, one way or another. But things fall apart. They fall apart a lot, and very quickly. I want to focus here on Philosophy as a discipline in its academic form, particularly in the UK and US, before turning to some of the claims made in the recent Xenofeminist manifesto[2] and the Gender Nihilism anti-manifesto[3] regarding the feminizing of reason and the abolition of gender. I will ultimately agree with the Xenofeminist manifesto when it states that "[r]ationalism must itself be a feminism" and with the Gender Nihilist text when it argues that the subversion of gender is a dead-end. I want only to add

1   I have capitalized the word "Philosophy" throughout where I'm referring to it in its disciplinary, academic sense.
2   Laboria Cuboniks, "Xenofeminism: A Politics for Alienation," http://www.laboriacuboniks.net/qx8bq.txt.
3   phoenixsinger, "Gender Nihilism: An Anti-Manifesto," *libcom,* July 9, 2015, https://libcom.org/library/gender-nihilism-anti-manifesto.

that what usually gets sidelined and undermined as "emotion," and is frequently gendered as feminine or female, is *also* itself a rationalism, and that emotion and reason are in fact not mortal enemies, but rather inseparable branches of the collective experience of social and political life that Philosophy purports to address.

I want to focus on Philosophy in particular, not only because it is the subject I have studied since I was 18, nearly half my life, and taught in for the past ten years, as PhD student then as a lecturer. It is a subject and a way, or rather ways, of thinking that I have never left since I encountered it and it is hard to imagine I will move too far away from it, in whatever form that will take in the future. However, there is no doubt that Philosophy has a serious and a series of problems when it comes to sexism. A recent high-profile case, among many, concerns an American PhD student who had a relationship with a very high-profile moral philosopher. Towards the end of her anonymous account of her relationship with the philosopher, she addresses fears that he could sabotage her future career in the field, and reflects on the context in which Philosophy is taught at universities:

> As a PhD student about to enter the world of professional philosophy, I now know better what I'm getting into. My hero, who regularly uses and condemns sexist practices in his lectures, said that Person N is not a real feminist, because she wears miniskirts when she gives lectures. He sat around with other renowned philosophers from the prestigious university in City Z, grumbling about how a stupid woman does not deserve her new prestigious university post. Now I understand better what they mean when they say that academic philosophy is a white boys' club. I am barely starting my career, but my eyes are already wide open.[4]

4 Anonymous, "I had an Affair with my Hero, a Philosopher who's Famous for being 'Moral,'" April 26, 2014, http://thoughtcatalog.com/anonymous/2014/04/i-had-an-affair-with-my-hero-a-philosopher-whos-famous-for-being-moral/.

When we are talking about sexism in Philosophy, there are multiple ways of considering the issue:

1. The subject itself: is Philosophy as a subject inherently sexist (and we could add racist: this is a "white boys' club" as the student above notes)?
2. Is Philosophy sexist by omission, i.e., accidentally sexist, racist and that with a bit of work "the numbers" could improve over time?
3. Is Philosophy only contingently sexist in a different way, because of misconceptions relating to what the subject is — too difficult, too belligerent, etc.?

In her important 1982 essay, "Woman as Body: Ancient and Contemporary Views," Elizabeth Spelman accuses Philosophy of a combination of somatophobia — that is, hatred of the body — and misogyny, as it is women who tend to be associated with the "loathed" body by male philosophers. Her focus, in part, is Plato and the mind/body distinction as it is this key division that sets the tone for much of what historically follows. She writes:

> How a philosopher conceives of the distinction and relation between soul (or mind) and body has essential ties to how that philosopher talks about the nature of knowledge, the accessibility of reality, the possibility of freedom. This is perhaps what one would expect — systematic connections among the "proper" philosophical issues addressed by a given philosopher. But there is also clear evidence in the philosophical texts of the relationship between [how] the mind/body distinction, is drawn, on the one hand, and the scattered official and unofficial utterances about the nature of women, on the other.[5]

5   Elizabeth V. Spelman, "Woman as Body: Ancient and Contemporary Views," *Feminist Studies* 8, no. 1 (Spring 1982): 109–31, at 110.

Here Spelman makes a conceptual connection between Philosophy as a subject and misogyny — Philosophy as a subject is inherently anti-woman, because many male philosophers are. Women are implicitly or explicitly aligned with the body by Philosophy, leaving the mind/soul to be elevated above its bearer. The conceptual is personal.

Can we bring Spelman's argument about ancient thought to bear on today's questioning concerning the discipline of Philosophy and sexism? Can we explain why there are still so few women in Philosophy — numbers after undergraduate degrees (where 46% are women in the UK) drop off sharply with only around 29% of PhDs and 20% of permanent post-holders in Philosophy being women — putting it on a comparable level with maths, physics, and computer science — and very dissimilar number-wise to English and History.[6] So it is clear that women in the first place aren't put off from studying the subject, but something happens at postgraduate level and beyond. Some have argued that Philosophy is off-putting because it is overtly combative, pedantic, and critical (although this wouldn't explain why a large number of female students choose to take the subject in the first place). Jonathan Wolff, UCL Philosophy Professor, in an article entitled: "How Can We End the Male Domination of Philosophy?" makes this well-worn argument and concludes by suggesting that "if philosophy is to be more 'gender friendly', do philosophers have first to act, well, if not in more 'ladylike' fashion, then at least with greater decorum?"[7] I find this suggestion somewhat patronizing, and the assumption that philosophers equal male in the first place unhelpful — I don't believe that women are inherently interested in "greater decorum" and certainly not when it comes to engaging with

6   See the careful report "Women in Philosophy in the UK: A Report by the British Philosophical Association and the Society for Women in Philosophy," Sept. 2011, http://www.bpa.ac.uk/uploads/2011/02/BPA_Report_Women_In_Philosophy.pdf.

7   Jonathan Wolff, "How Can We End the Male Domination of Philosophy?," *The Guardian,* Nov. 26, 2013, http://www.theguardian.com/education/2013/nov/26/modern-philosophy-sexism-needs-more-women.

philosophical arguments. Certainly, I have encountered many male philosophers who behave unpleasantly, but this is because they appear to believe that as Philosophers they have a get-out-of-jail-free card regarding any kind of "normal" social behavior (civility, respect, compassion). But this has nothing to do with how we might argue *within* the discipline: it is perfectly possible to repeatedly enter a human bear pit and be a kind and gentle person as well — the problem is the social stuff, not necessarily the discipline stuff. But as someone who has never acted "ladylike," nor do I think most women have, *not least because it doesn't mean anything,* I wonder about the value of promoting decorum *inside* the discipline: more important, perhaps, would be not acting in a hostile and dismissive manner to anyone perceived to be outside of it.

Hovering in the background of all this is a murky conglomeration of stereotypes and received wisdom. The British Philosophical Association and Society for Women in Philosophy joint report from 2011 suggests that

> The point here is not that women are somehow less able to cope when aggressive behaviour is aimed at them, and so should be treated more gently than men. It is rather that aggressive behaviour, whoever it is aimed at, can heighten women's feeling that they do not belong by reinforcing the masculine nature of the environment within which they study and work.[8]

This is a clever and more subtle way of addressing a key issue — what does it mean to be constantly interpolated as an anomaly? What is masculinity in the context of Philosophy anyway? The problem here is less the stereotypes concerning women in Philosophy and more the unacknowledged, because faux-neutral, acceptability of tropes associated with masculinity. What happens when you stick out in this context? As the report states: "Stereotype threat is likely to be provoked where one is from a group that is negatively stigmatized in a certain

8   "Women In Philosophy in the UK," 13.

21

context, one is in that context, and one's group membership is made salient,"[9] i.e., being one of only a few women in a roomful of men is sufficient to make one's group membership salient. Given that this is routinely the case in Philosophy departments, I think recent efforts to identify stereotypes working the other way serve a useful function.

The jokey term "theory boy" has been around for a while, but serves to identify a specificity that usually passes itself off as a generality. As Toril Moi puts it in "Discussion or Aggression? Arrogance and Despair in Graduate School" from 2003, "Among graduate students there is often a feeling of depression, as if out of humiliation, or a feeling of disappointment, as if out of arrogance."[10] She writes:

> Every year some female graduate students tell me that they feel overlooked, marginalized, silenced in some seminars. They paint a picture of classrooms where the alpha males — so-called "theory boys" — are encouraged to hold forth in impossibly obscure language, but where their own interventions elicit no response.[11]

Moi describes this situation in terms of symbolic capital, and following Bourdieu, describes "the relentless fight to become 'consecrated' as one of the legitimate heirs to institutional power and glory."[12] To become the heir of the concept appears to mean in practice the exclusion of those who are deemed to not belong to concepts as such — in this sense then, those marked out as "women" and non-white males are perpetually registered as being particular, rather than universal, even when making points in the "appropriate register." They cannot be heard because no one wants to listen. There is a kind of "double bind" of the uni-

9   Ibid.

10   Toril Moi, "Discussion or Aggression? Arrogance and Despair in Graduate School," *The Grind: Duke School Graduate Magazine* (July 2003): 1, http://www.torilmoi.com/wp-content/uploads/2009/09/Moi_Arrogance-and-despair_2003.pdf.

11   Ibid., 2.

12   Ibid., 1.

versal at play here, where those deemed minoritarian (even if, in a global sense, this isn't true) are encouraged to "play by the rules," to become bearers of the universal, the enlightened, the conceptual, the theoretical, for their own good and for the good of humanity as a whole. However, if they do they are somehow both no longer minoritarian (as any particularism magically vanishes) but also not really true players either, because suddenly the person sitting on the other side of the board has disappeared.

The recent "Xenofeminism Manifesto" (2015) takes up the challenge of the relationship between rationalism and universalism declaring that:

> Xenofeminism is a rationalism. To claim that reason or rationality is "by nature" a patriarchal enterprise is to concede defeat. It is true that the canonical "history of thought" is dominated by men, and it is male hands we see throttling existing institutions of science and technology. But this is precisely why feminism must be a rationalism — because of this miserable imbalance, and not despite it. There is no "feminine" rationality, nor is there a "masculine" one. Science is not an expression but a suspension of gender. If today it is dominated by masculine egos, then it is at odds with itself — and this contradiction can be leveraged. Reason, like information, wants to be free, and patriarchy cannot give it freedom. Rationalism must itself be a feminism. XF marks the point where these claims intersect in a two-way dependency. It names reason as an engine of feminist emancipation, and declares the right of everyone to speak as no one in particular.[13]

While both acknowledging rationalism's male domination, and the way in which this holds science back, as well as the un-gendering, de-gendering, or a-gendering qualities of science, the Xenofeminist Manifesto nevertheless hankers after the voice from nowhere represented by the final line: "the right of everyone to speak as no one in particular." What is the relationship

13 Cuboniks, "Xenofeminism," 0x04.

between speaking "as" no one and speaking from a marginalized position? Can we not do both? Feminist scientists and feminist philosophers of science are no less universalist or rationalist than male scientists, but they do not pretend to be speaking from nowhere, and, indeed, it is their feminist commitments that often reveal precisely what has been overlooked in earlier research. Patricia Gowaty, to give just one example, revolution-ized the way in which aviary sexuality was conceived in her work on extra pair copulations and intraspecific egg dumping because she focussed less on male birds' cuckoldry and more on the strategies of the female birds she was studying.[14]

Another recent piece, "Gender Nihilism: An Anti-Manifes-to" recently appeared online.[15] Like the Xenofeminist Manifesto it is anonymously authored (the Xenofeminist manifesto is per-haps less anonymous than this piece, given the six-part collec-tive name "Laboria Cubonics" and some high-profile associa-tions with the text) and perhaps collectively written (certainly the use of "we" as authorial voice would indicate this). Like the Xenofeminist Manifesto, the Gender Nihilism Anti-Manifesto rejects essentialism of any kind, right through to the ontological realm: "Who we are, the very core of our being, might perhaps not be found in the categorical realm of being at all."[16] Both the Xenofeminists and the Gender Nihillists declare themselves "gender abolitionists," but while the former argue that the actual eradication of "gendered" traits under patriarchy "could only spell disaster" and suggest instead, in a slightly techno-hippie way, that we should let "a hundred sexes bloom!," the Gender Nihilists go much further, arguing instead that:

> We are radicals who have had enough with attempts to salvage gen-der. We do not believe we can make it work for us. We look at the

14 See Michelle Elekonich, "Contesting Territories: Female-Female Aggres-sion and the Song Sparrow," in *Feminist Science Studies: A New Generation,* eds. Maralee Mayberry, Banu Subramaniam, and Lisa H. Weasel (London: Routledge, 2001), 103.

15 phoenixsinger, "Gender Nihilism: An Anti-Manifesto."

16 Ibid.

transmisogyny we have faced in our own lives, the gendered violence that our comrades, both trans and cis have faced, and we realize that the apparatus itself makes such violence inevitable.[17]

And, as if in response to the Xenofeminists' blooming of the
sexes argument, suggest that in the current moment "it becomes
tempting to embrace a certain liberal politics of expansion [...].
We have heard the suggestion that non-binary identity, trans
identity, and queer identity might be able to create a subversion of gender. This cannot be the case"[18] and furthermore, that
"[i]nfinite gender identities create infinite new spaces of devia-
tion which will be violently punished."[19] There are similarities
between the two texts, though, particularly around what the
Xenofeminist text describes as "the right of everyone to speak
as no one in particular." As the Gender Nihilism text states: "it
is not merely certain formulations of identity politics which
we seek to combat, but the need for identity altogether." While
there may be subtle differences between speaking as the generic "nobody" and speaking from the position of the abolition
of identity, there is a parallel need for an escape route from an
overcoded set of identifications deemed to be partial from the
standpoint of a universal that fails to recognize its own specificity (for how else could we describe masculinity)?

How then can the gender nihilist and the Xenofeminist positions help us understand what happens in Philosophy? If we understand "gendered violence" to include what often takes place
within the discipline, we can understand that to try to make
the subject more palatable for other genders on the basis of stereotypes about people gendered in these ways (women are less
combative, let's make the subject more approachable) are highly
likely to fail, even where they are attempted, which is nowhere.
Far better might be to operate under conditions of extreme
transparency and a comprehension of the operations of domi-

17   Ibid.
18   Ibid.
19   Ibid.

nance. As the anti-manifesto puts it: "The gender nihilist says 'I am a woman' and means that they are located within a certain position in a matrix of power which constitutes them as such."[20]

But how does rationalism overall fare in the Xenofeminist and gender abolitionist universe? What would a rationalism stripped of its masculinist history look like? I want to claim that this rationalism must also be an emotionalism, that is to say, a neglect of the *rational* basis for anger, misery, hatred, love, care, and so on will likely end up reinstating old oppositions and with them, gendered presuppositions about where thought "belongs." Spinoza in the *Ethics* already teaches us this. And this understanding, above all, a social question, a practical question. As Ericka Tucker puts it in "Spinoza's Social Sage": "Few, if any, communities are organized through reason alone. Affects and the imagination are the primary modes through which humans interact and join their power."[21] Gender is the violence done to both reason and emotion by virtue of separating the two along sexed lines. Philosophy need not be the victim of this.

But where are we now? As the Xenofeminists suggest at the moment "the notion of what is 'gendered' sticks disproportionately to the feminine."[22] It follows then, that Philosophy must not become more "ladylike," whatever that might mean, but must abolish and overturn the oppositions (mind–body, emotion–reason) that have sustained its endeavor as protector of a masculinized set of knowledges and methodologies. Philosophy is not "hard" because it makes a particular subsection of humanity feel strengthened in their identity-that-pretends-not-to-be-one, but because life is hard, and Philosophy should address its difficulties openly and collectively.

---

20 Ibid.
21 Ericka Tucker, "Spinoza's Social Sage: Emotion and the Power of Reason in Spinoza's Social Theory," *Revista Conatus* (July 2015): 12.
22 Cuboniks, "Xenofeminist Manifesto," 0x0E.

The Other Woman

Katherine Behar

> *This is why we can't have nice things.*
> — Anonymous

Not-So-Nice Things

Recent new realist theories intend to respect objects by leaving them to their own "weird" ways.[1] However, in seeking to rethink how objects access each other, and how humans have access to the world, these philosophies consistently center on questions of having access to things or, put simply, having them.[2] Ultimately, there is something perversely exotic about objects

I am grateful to Irina Aristarkhova, Anne Pollock, and Trevor Smith, who offered feedback on early drafts of this paper, and to Angela Valenti and Lisa Delgado for their support of this project. I owe great thanks to Silvia Federici, for generously sharing her research archive, and to Arlen Austen, for his archival help.

1   For a compendium of speculative realist thought, which often takes this approach, see *The Speculative Turn,* eds. Levi Bryant, Nick Srnicek, and Graham Harman (Melbourne: re.press, 2011). See also Graham Harman's term "weird realism" in *Weird Realism: Lovecraft and Philosophy* (Alresford: Zero Books, 2012), and Timothy Morton's "magical" take on realism in *Realist Magic: Objects, Ontology, Causality* (Ann Arbor: Open Humanities Press, 2013).

2   Consider, for example, how noncorrelationism, Quentin Meillassoux's founding gesture for speculative realism, claims the possibility of having access to being in-itself, apart from thought. Quentin Meillassoux, *After Fini-*

framed, through the language of object-orientation, as a form of alterity that is meant to be *had* even if from afar. This dynamic carries sexual undertones and is entangled in objectification and reification. Any fetishist will attest that weirdness can be sexy, and this holds true, it would appear, even in philosophy. Whether or not one chooses to read terms like *allure* and *withdrawal* as flirtatious or frigid, attributing distant availability to objects produces what I call an exoticism of objects. As we will see, this exoticism troubles economies of access and having, which I contend are foundational for new realist philosophies.

In considering these ideas, I will be drawing on emerging discourses in object-oriented feminism.[3] Like the object-oriented philosophies that have proliferated in the wake of speculative realism, which collectively insist that the universe is composed of objects and that humans are objects like all others, object-oriented feminism embraces nonanthropocentrism. It also pursues a feminist ethical stake in the histories and implications of objectification, which today's object-oriented theories may have occasion to renew. In "Treating Objects Like Women," Timothy Morton states that the term *object* does "not stand for objectification or reification."[4] His "weird essentialism" recuperates "the supposed biological essentialism of French and 1970s American feminism," torquing an unfashionable phase of feminist analysis toward the worthy project of object-oriented feminist ecology.

tude: An Essay on the Necessity of Contingency, trans. Ray Brassier (2006; rpt.London: Continuum, 2008).

3   Object-oriented feminism (OOF) is a new field of analysis that has been developing out of several years of panels I organized at annual meetings of the Society for Literature, Science, and the Arts, and dialogues around a forthcoming edited volume, *Object-Oriented Feminism,* ed. Katherine Behar (Minneapolis: University of Minnesota Press, 2016). Among the authors in this volume, Patricia Ticineto Clough and Frenchy Lunning have been actively involved in developing OOF thought since its inception, and editor Eileen A. Joy was an OOF panel respondent in 2012.

4   Timothy Morton, "Treating Objects Like Women: Feminist Ontology and the Question of Essence," in *International Perspectives in Feminist Ecocriticism,* eds. Greta Gaard, Serpil Opperman, and Simon Estok (New York: Routledge, 2013), 56–69, at 56.

But perhaps Morton is too hasty in dismissing objects' imbrication in objectification and reification. Object-oriented feminism is directly concerned with treating humans like things. Equally, it is engaged in extending intra-human feminist ethics to the object world and in cultivating posthuman solidarities.

In this context, an important aspect of object-oriented feminism's ethical challenge can be posed as an inversion of the speculative question of how humans have access to things. Instead, object-oriented feminism takes up a thing's perspective and asks how things are had. This essay will address such questions of access and having by way of a provocative human object, the "other woman," to arrive at a proposal for object-oriented feminist erotics.[5] An alternative to "aesthetics as first philosophy," object-oriented feminist erotics undermines the principle of value in aesthetics and in productivist relationships between objects. But first let us assess how having access to things, having things, and having one's way with things have been playing out in new realist philosophies thus far.

Having at Things

One way philosophers have at things is through metaphor. For example, in Graham Harman's non-relational philosophy, metaphor summons real objects together toward access. Harman theorizes that objects have no access to each other because they are fundamentally "withdrawn."[6] Each object, he claims, is its own world, hermetically, ontologically, and prophylactically "vacuum-sealed." Harman proposes a novel concept he calls "al-

---

5   This object of analysis, like the title of this essay, references Luce Irigaray's *Speculum of the Other Woman*; however, beyond a rich point of inspiration, Irigaray's text is not a primary focus for this short essay. See *Speculum of the Other Woman,* trans. Gillian C. Gill (1974; rpt. Ithaca: Cornell University Press, 1985). On the connection between masculinist speculation as theorized by Irigaray and its significance for feminist philosophy "after the 'speculative turn,'" see Katerina Kolozova's Preface to this volume.

6   Graham Harman, "On Vicarious Causation," in *Collapse Vol. II: Speculative Realism,* ed. R. Mackay (2007; rpt. Falmouth: Urbanomic, 2012), 215.

lure" to account for the reality of influence and dynamism in the universe, notwithstanding his notion of withdrawal.

Allure is the metaphoric process by which qualities from one object are applied figuratively to another. In the construct of allure, reticent, "withdrawn" objects are coaxed into "connection" in order to fertilize change or "vicarious" incidents of causality, while still remaining wholly apart from each other. To add an analogy of my own, allure is akin to dressing in drag. An alluring object remains of-itself but with the addition of qualities borrowed from another object, which surface without making the first object's core being any less withdrawn; in fact, these borrowed qualities even allude to something unknowable beneath that very surface.

This arrangement constitutes the foundation of Harman's aesthetics, which he claims as first philosophy.[7] Surprisingly, considering this prominence, the term *allure* is loaded with innuendo. Among other things, allure is likely to summon sultry ads for a Chanel perfume, or feminine wiles instructed by a Condé Nast beauty magazine, both of which bear its name. Harman explains that allure involves allusion, so such associations with feminized products of patriarchy are not accidental; its connotation is itself an example of the process he has in mind. In other words, it is a function of allure when *allure* becomes as suggestive as the enticingly vacant gaze of a languorous model positioned beside a bottle of French perfume.

Even setting aside Harman's penchant for flamboyant prose, the scent of seduction and conquest permeates his terminology.[8] For Harman, allure "alludes to entities as they are, quite apart from any relations with or effects upon other entities in the world," but some readers might conclude that allure also alludes

7   Graham Harman, "Aesthetics as First Philosophy: Levinas and the Non-Human," *Naked Punch* 9 (Summer/Fall 2007): 21–30.

8   Numerous examples exist throughout his oeuvre. To take but one instance, in the main passage from which I draw in this section, Harman invokes the image that a real object surrounded by sensual ones "pierces their colored mists" to connect with another real object nearby. See Harman, "On Vicarious Causation," 213.

to sexual courtship.[9] Against withdrawal's surly non-relation, allure offers a bewitching whiff to suggest things could get interesting as withdrawn objects beckon each other.[10] Even Harman's chosen example for the metaphoric transfer of qualities through allure is romantic: the poet's pronouncement "my heart is a furnace."[11]

For his part, Morton associates an object's withdrawal with its essence, or irreducibility.[12] Thus, an object's withdrawn essence accounts for allure. Objects are "essentially" alluring, and here we would do well to recall the biological essentialism Morton has evoked in his "weird" version, and its association

9   Graham Harman, "The Well-Wrought Broken Hammer: Object-Oriented Literary Criticism," *New Literary History* 43, no. 2 (Spring 2012): 183–207, at 187.

10 Different flavors of object-oriented philosophy speculate differently on the finer points of non-relation. For example, Levi Bryant describes a "democracy of objects" composing a "flat ontology" that stresses horizontal adjacency rather than separation; Bruno Latour conceives of objects as networked actors; and Ian Bogost, like many object-oriented feminists, typically explores objects of a cultural, artificial nature, inherently tinged by or even arising from other objects' meddling. Yet still in the title of a book like *Alien Phenomenology, or What It's Like to Be a Thing* (riffing on Thomas Nagel's 1974 essay, "What Is It Like to Be a Bat?") Bogost maintains the air of alien foreignness and aloof unintelligibility in objects' presentations to each other. Likewise, consider Morton's account of objects' self-differing as an internal "looping" structure. Twisting away from self-identification, Morton's looping objects (and his rolling prose) are curvaceous and tantalizing — even while hinting at juvenile infatuation, evoked by a "Looney Tunes" overture. In object-oriented feminism, all objects are indeed set in such suggestive motion, wavering seductively between attraction and repulsion. See Levi R. Bryant, *The Democracy of Objects* (Ann Arbor: Open Humanities Press, 2011); Bruno Latour, *Reassembling the Social: An Introduction to Actor-Network-Theory* (New York: Oxford University Press, 2005); Graham Harman, *Prince of Networks: Bruno Latour and Metaphysics* (Melbourne: re.press, 2009); Ian Bogost, *Alien Phenomenology, or What It's Like to Be a Thing* (Minneapolis, University of Minnesota Press, 2012); and Timothy Morton, "All Objects Are Deviant: Feminism and Ecological Intimacy," in *Object-Oriented Feminism*.

11 Harman, "On Vicarious Causation," 215–16.

12 Morton, "Treating Objects Like Women," 59.

with female bodies. For not only furnace-like hearts but bodies themselves can speak metaphoric volumes.

Frenchy Lunning insightfully connects the shared use of metaphor in Harman's notion of allure with Julia Kristeva's concept of the abject to draw the body of an "other" woman, the menstruating and even postmenopausal body of the older woman, into the feminist fold.[13] For Harman, metaphor constitutes what Lunning calls a "come hither" gesture soliciting the otherness of withdrawn other objects. But if, as in a perfume ad, allure is associated with the pubescent, attractive young girl whose nubile body suggests her availability or have-ability, Lunning perceives its complement in Kristeva's metaphor for abjection as a "violent repulsing thrusting aside of 'otherness.'" In this gestural reversal, alluring femininity becomes one of Harman's severed qualities, shoved off and overcoded into abjection in the figure of the mother, "the defining subject/object position for females, which is necessarily thrust aside." Lunning captures this inverted fusion of allure and abjection, and its significance for object-oriented feminism, in the following passage:

> This leaves the emerging female subject/object in a rather sticky spot, especially under patriarchal conditions. For under the patriarchy, women are reduced to various image objects of their singular and necessary function of reproduction: not just the mother, but also the bodacious babe who is codified and commodified in terms of breeding potential. As such, women are abjected and degraded as objects in all senses of the word, and so is any linkage with the maternal and feminine objects in the culture. The coded trappings of feminine objects — the notes of these objects — and especially those clustered around the extreme manifestations of feminine qualities, are thus regarded as cloying, obnoxious, and disgusting objects.[14]

13 Frenchy Lunning, "Allure and Abjection: The Possible Potential of Severed Qualities," in *Object-Oriented Feminism.*

14 Ibid.

Of course, it is also the abject older woman, the madame, who provides access to another kind of "other woman": prostitutes. Not coincidentally, when Harman attempts to arrange the meeting of objects, he posits a third enveloping facilitator object, which in effect assumes the role of the madame, providing a space where two objects can meet on neutral turf to engage. "My claim," he writes, "is that two entities influence one another only by meeting on the interior of a third, where they exist side-by-side until something happens that allows them to interact."[15] Abject or alluring, this enveloping intentional object conjures the conspicuous interior of the madame's abject environment.

Things to Have and Things to Hold

We cannot ignore the uneasy relations binding objects in object-oriented philosophy to objectification and reification. In the red light district's rosy glow, objectification, labor, gender, and class bathe in the same light. Here, object-oriented feminism links Harman's invocation of tools to biopolitical histories of use, exploitation, and resistance. In his reading of Heidegger, Harman explains that the world consists of two types of objects: tools, which are "ready-to-hand," and broken tools, which are "present-at-hand." By flouting the human intention of use, the latter confront their masters, hinting at the depths of their full, glorious, uncolonizable strangeness. What Harman calls "tool being" is distinguished by exploitation and resistance. In object-oriented feminism, exploitation names the treatment of tools through use, misuse, and abuse, and resistance designates the opposing behavior of broken tools that defy being so treated.

If all objects are either tools or broken tools, let us consider two human objects of interest for feminist philosophy, the "wife" objectified as property, and the sex worker reified as the "other woman" in a most bare form. How are we to understand these women/objects as broken/tools? My purpose is not to reiterate a tired binary between Madonnas and whores. On the contrary,

15   Harman, "On Vicarious Causation," 190.

33

I want to seriously weigh the contention that all objects, including humans, and hence including women, are at once captured in and resistant to confining systems of labor and possession.

The Marxist feminist movement Wages for Housework exemplifies this predicament. Building on a history of women's mobilizing for financial independence, the movement rose to international prominence in the 1970s, the same era when many feminists also adopted strategic essentialism. Wages for Housework reasoned that it was unjust (and unsafe) for women to remain financially dependent on their husbands because wifely housework was indispensable reproductive labor without which the capitalist system could not survive.

Silvia Federici recounts how, in an 1876 letter to the editor, a Kentucky housewife made precisely this argument.[16] The response from the editor of *The New York Times,* reproaching the woman for so much as mentioning money, exposes the continuity between a wife's work, and an "other woman's" labor.

> If women wish the position of wife to have the honor which they attach to it, they will not talk about the value of their services and about stated incomes, but they will live with their husbands in the spirit of the vow cf. the English marriage service, taking them "for better; for worse; for richer, for poorer; in sickness and in health; to love, honor, and obey." This it is to be a wife; and not to be this, and not to be willing to share a man's fortunes and give him the respect and submission due to the master of a household, is to take on a perilous likeness to women in certain other relations, who do demand stated incomes, or at least wages, and whose position is such that there is always at least reasonable doubt as to their right to talk to a man about their care of "his" children.[17]

16 Silvia Federici presented this material at "Wages for Housework," a workshop held at The Commons Brooklyn on Saturday, March 21, 2015.

17 See "Wives' Wages," *The New York Times,* August 10, 1876, quoted in Silvia Federici, *Revolution at Point Zero: Housework, Reproduction, and Feminist Struggle* (Oakland: PM Press, 2012), 41.

Tools behave nicely. They are demure. They present themselves for service retiringly, to be used without reward. We can have our way with tools because they don't warrant our second thought. But there is something altogether wrong with the broken tool. It is not a nice thing at all. Broken tools disturb our contentment, stand out brashly, and demand our attention. So what kind of woman claims remuneration for her work? What insolence turns a woman from a useful tool, resigned to her cultural role, into a broken one, requiring recognition? A sex worker is an easy target for being objectified and reified as a would-be human sex toy. But, is only the "other woman" used as a tool? Or, is the wife used as a tool until she "breaks" and demands her fair pay? Or, is her broken demand precisely what threatens to reclassify her as mere tool, as an "other woman" and no longer an esteemed wife? Clearly broken tools can't account for these other women abounding, breaking things and the economy of being had. The tool analysis doesn't fit nicely.

What We Can't Have

Let us be clear: the unshakeable problem with viewing the world as tools and broken tools is that this thinking leaves the Hegelian dynamic of servitude intact. The real issue for object-oriented feminism is not the difference between tools and broken tools but the power differential between users and tools, masters and slaves.[18]

To be a tool is to be in the service of another. And so, Harman protests what he perceives as the servile position of most contemporary philosophy, which he laments "grovels at [science's] feet. 'How may I serve thee, master?'"[19] Harman's refrain is that

18 I explore the philosophic and sexual dynamics of mastery and servitude among human users and nonhuman tools in Katherine Behar, "Command and Control: Cybernetics and BDSM," in *Digital Arts and Culture 2009 Proceedings* (Irvine: University of California Irvine, 2009), http://escholarship. org/uc/item/42r1836z.

19 Andrew Iliadis, "Interview with Graham Harman (2)," *Figure/Ground*, http://figureground.org/interview-with-graham-harman-2/.

philosophy should pursue reality in its own right and must not be the "handmaid" of any other discipline. Promoting aesthetics as first philosophy, he views recalibrating philosophic priorities to account for the significance of his concept of allure as a gallant move, by which he stands ready to rescue aesthetics from scandalous, perhaps whorish, ruin. Here not only handmaids but also dancing girls populate his rousing calls to philosophers. "Until now," Harman writes, "aesthetics has generally served as the impoverished dancing-girl of philosophy — admired for her charms, but no gentleman would marry her." [20]

Adding up these accounts, which seem to be overflowing with unacknowledged feminine metaphors (and patriarchal baggage), object-oriented feminists might easily arrive at erotics, not aesthetics, as first philosophy. [21] Harman maintains that his philosophy does not promote a method, but a countermethod. But erotics might well be object-oriented feminism's method, if only to lay waste to toolish propositions like these.

Having One's Way with Things

Erotics erodes boundaries between self and other, as well as the complementarity that upholds the master–slave dialectic by requiring the integrity of each of these figures delimited as humanist subjects. When object-oriented feminism advocates feminist solidarity across all objects in all manner of erotic coalitions, it is in order to recognize objects' shared servitude under dominant relations of production. The work things do dissolves seeming separations between human sex workers and nonhuman sex toys, *as well as* apparent oppositions between wives and "other women." As broken/tools, sex workers, sex toys, and wives are all implemented in physical and affective labor in the service of social reproduction.

20 Harman, "On Vicarious Causation," 216.
21 I expand on this concept in "An Introduction to OOF," developing the notion of erotics in object-oriented feminism through the work of Audre Lorde, Georges Bataille, and others. See Katherine Behar, "An Introduction to OOF," in *Object-Oriented Feminism.*

According to Jean Baudrillard's concept of "seduction," all three are reduced to masculine value, having lost the viability of feminine uncertainty, which here I would relate to the broken tool's capacity to surprise when it refuses to be had. For Baudrillard, capitalism represents how relations of production replace relations of seduction (which is not the same as the sexual, which is itself productivist). As Baudrillard warns, "it is women who are now about to lose, precisely under the sign of sexual pleasure," which is scrupulously productive, "mak[ing] everything speak, everything babble, everything climax." Baudrillard critiques the women's movement for advancing a sexual logic in its "promotion of the female as a sex in its own right (equal rights, equal pleasures), of the female as value — at the expense of the female as a principle of uncertainty."[22] We could say the same for object-oriented theories that seek to elevate objects as quasi-subjects. Ironically, such theories of things' agency and would-be weird volition will always be at the expense of erotic uncertainty. In economic positivity, things can be "had" in all senses of the word, so certainty also accompanies the exotic object of desire, which can be positively counted upon to remain always alluringly unattainable.

Evelyn Fox Keller frames the erotic in opposition to similar dominant practices in the sciences that seek mastery of nature and its objects. Describing this productivist mastery over objects, which Federici, Carolyn Merchant, and others connect to the dual exploitation of women and nature throughout the history of capitalism, precisely as an engine of such productivity, Fox Keller identifies "a degree of control that one would not think of having in relation to a subject that one had a more erotic, more interactive, more reciprocal feeling-engagement with."[23] Mastery abolishes the possibility of erotic uncertainty

---

22 Jean Baudrillard, *Seduction*, trans. Brian Singer (1979; rpt. Montreal: Ctheory Books, 2001), 20.

23 Evelyn Fox Keller and Bill Moyers, "Evelyn Fox Keller: The Gendered Language of Science" (transcript), *World of Ideas*, http://billmoyers.com/content/evelyn-fox-keller/.

because it involves definitive "control in the Baconian sense of domination, that nature is there to be steered, to be directed."[24]

Erotics lessens self/other distinctions. This means refusing the hierarchical separations of aesthetics, like the false separations that persist in the adjacent productivities of wives and mistresses, madames and dancing girls, philosophers and handmaids. In each of these couplings, ideological distinctions of not/niceness describe and generate value. Aesthetics functions on the same principle of difference, as do all systems of value. We value things for being nice instead of not — or vice versa — because value is always comparative, hinging on degrees of difference. Because erotics is an enemy of difference it is incompatible with value and all it entails. While master and slave reciprocally produce each other as discrete but productively intertwined identities, the erotic surrender of self-unto-other turns "having" an identity or "taking" a lover into "giving it up." Erotics reaches its zenith in the giving up of self-sacrifice, a becoming one with the universe that is comparable to the devastating expenditure of potlatch and tantamount to the death of the individual.

In more mundane terms, erotics also means simply this: We must overcome the insidious distancing from which metaphors overreach and within which exoticism lingers. In the total ontological scope of object-orientation, feminist struggle should not be about Hegelian recognition as becoming vis-à-vis the struggle to become a subject instead of an object or a master instead of a slave. (Nor should it be about becoming a slave instead of a master or an object instead of a subject.) These distinctions only perpetuate productivism, reinstating capitalist systems of value generation, labor, and utilitarian possession. What remains for feminists and other women is to erotically disable dialectic complementarities like these.

24 Ibid.

Libérer épistémologiquement le féminisme

Anne-Françoise Schmid

Introduction : des humain(e)s et de la science

Peut-on mettre en rapport la recherche des critères de scientificité et les études sur le genre ? Y a-t-il des raisons de rapporter la façon d'identifier la science à un sexe plutôt qu'à un autre ? Les deux questions peuvent sembler éloignées, mais elles sont mises en tension par un fait général : les critères de la science ont été recherchés de façon systématique au siècle où la situation de la femme s'est, dans nos pays occidentaux, nettement améliorée du point de vue de l'accès à la connaissance et à l'exercice d'une profession scientifique. Dans le moment où l'on cherchait des règles pour reconnaître la science de ce qui n'est pas science, les femmes ont pris une place effective, non exceptionnelle, dans les études scientifiques et philosophiques. Y a-t-il un rapport entre ces deux mouvements ? L'échec de la recherche de ces critères universels, qui sont maintenant reconnus comme ayant une valeur locale, les modifications au concept d'objectivité qu'il a provoquées, peuvent-ils avoir des conséquences sur l'ouverture aux femmes de l'accès aux sciences ?

Il n'y a pas de réponse directe. Le « oui » et le « non » peuvent aller l'un et l'autre de soi en philosophie en fonction de la position que l'on a et que l'on cherche à défendre. Oui, les femmes ont changé les choses par une pratique différente des sciences — mais en quoi tient cette différence ? Et qu'entend-on par différence ? Non, les sciences ont une telle forme d'autonomie par rapport aux autres savoirs, que la différence des sexes ne peut y avoir de prise — mais qu'entend-on alors par autonomie ? Quelque chose qui résisterait aux différences ? Toutes ces argumentations s'appuient sur des données qui peuvent paraître « vraies », mais que l'on peut pourtant retourner. S'il n'y a pas de réponse directe, il est par contre possible de changer de logique et concernant l'identité de la science et les rapports entre hommes et femmes. Avec l'abandon des critères universels (vérification, réfutation, programme de recherche, etc.), il est possible de mettre en rapport le concept de science avec les études sur le genre. Mais cela demande un changement théorique radical, celui de ne plus traiter philosophiquement les rapports de l'homme et de la femme en terme de différence et d'identité, mais de les combiner en tant que variables qui participent l'une et l'autre à la production d'une science déconstruite dans son approche épistémologique classique. La modification la plus importante est que la femme ne soit plus une surdétermination d'une science supposée masculine, avec toutes les protestations et les répétitions d'une lutte mutuelle et spéculaire.

Science classique et surdétermination par la femme

Les travaux féministes sur la philosophie des sciences ont en effet, la plupart du temps, ajouté des caractéristiques à la conception classique des sciences pour faire une place aux femmes. Prenons le concept de science, son objectivité, son sérieux, son autorité et ajoutons la connaissance située, le contexte, le point de vue, l'empirique, la narrativité, le pluralisme, l'hétérogénéité, les valeurs et nous pourrons construire une philosophie des sciences compatible avec une certaine idée de la femme sans nuire à l'objectivité scientifique. Mais c'est supposer que la science est masculine, et que sa mise en situation, en contexte et en récit est plutôt féminine. La femme ajouterait des caractéristiques à l'origine considérées comme non essentielles à la démarche scientifique, puisque celle-ci semblait invariante lorsqu'on l'extrayait de son contexte historique et social. Ainsi, la femme sur-déterminerait le concept de science en lui ajoutant des liens avec un milieu. Ce sont ces liens et leur diversité qui apparaîtraient comme féminins.

Notre approche est différente. La mise en tension des deux questions du début sur les critères et le genre est résolue de façon plus douce et plus large par une logique de sous-détermination que de sur-détermination. C'est la logique même de l'ajout de propriétés liées au genre que nous cherchons à modifier. Mais c'est également un mode de reconnaissance de la science jugé unique et objectif que nous transformons en vision partielle et locale de la science. Nous proposons donc un double mouvement où seraient engagés à la fois les humain(e)s et les sciences de façon plus élémentaire et moins sur-déterminée.

Premier stade : un féminisme ouvert et sans opposition

Au début du féminisme, il y a avait sans doute sens à montrer l'aspect culturel des différences sexuelles et d'en faire un enjeu. Il y a eu bien des aléas dans la lutte des femmes, et sans doute les acquis ne sont jamais tout à fait définitifs. Cette lutte repose sur une souffrance, qui n'est jamais complètement adoucie. Elle reprendra sous diverses formes, sera parfois étouffée ou mise en retrait. Cela est normal. Ce qui importe est que cette lutte ait eu lieu, parce que, à partir d'elle, il est possible de poser les problèmes autrement.

Nous ne reprenons pas cette lutte dans sa continuité. Nous n'allons pas, en fonction de cette lutte et de ses suites historiques, argumenter pour l'homme ou pour la femme. Par exemple, nous n'argumenterons pas sur le nombre de femmes devenues scientifiques et ingénieurs, comme de très nombreux travaux l'ont fait et continueront à le faire de façon très utile et tout à fait nécessaire pour qu'une certaine souffrance ne retourne pas en sa caverne. Notre question est plutôt, du fait de cette lutte, de traiter sans opposition femme et homme vis-à-vis de la science et de défaire cette opposition de type philosophique. Notre lutte, plutôt que contre l'homme, cherche à modifier une certaine idée de la femme, et donc en même temps une certaine idée de l'homme, que nous ne considérons pas comme fixes. D'autre part, tout en admettant la pertinence des débats sur l'objectivité scientifique et la remise en cause des critères, il s'agit de traiter la science comme ayant malgré tout une forme d'identité, et ne se diluant pas dans les luttes sociales. Les concepts d'identité et de différence sont-ils les bons pour traiter de l'implication de ces deux problèmes ? Comment les transformer, les rendre apte à ne pas relancer la guerre ? Pour cela, il ne faut plus qu'ils puissent s'échanger les uns dans les autres. Il faut une distinction encore différente de celle proposée dans certaines études sur le genre, du sexe biologique et du genre, historique, social, psychologique. Nous ne voulons en effet pas traiter la question par touches psychologiques, ajoutant des nuances à un donné déjà et trop bien connu. Nous proposons une autre distinction, plus radicale, parce que sans réversibilité possible, celle de l'humain(e) et du sujet, la première sans qualités, la seconde produite par les rapports entre les qualités et l'humain. Si nous traitons l'homme et la femme comme variables de façon égalitaire, nous ne pouvons plus dire ceci est un homme et ceci est une femme dans une logique de l'attribution, où « homme » et « femme » sont donnés et connus. Par les variables, ils sont transformés en « X », qui ne détruit pas les données, mais les enrichit de mondes et de propriétés différentes, les environne de connaissances beaucoup plus variées et riches.

Il faut admettre qu'il y a des hommes, qu'il y a des femmes, sans relancer les hiérarchies, qu'il y a de la science, qu'il y a de la philosophie, sans que l'on puisse les mettre en continuité et en réversibilité. La question n'est plus *entre* l'homme et la femme, entre la science et la philosophie, elle est plutôt celle d'un milieu, qui ne dépend directement ni des uns ni des autres. Il faut créer des espaces d'invention de ces notions, et ne plus les prendre comme définitivement données. Cet espace, que nous appelons générique, est construit dans ce rapport non réversible de l'humain(e) au sujet.

Deux propositions qui déplacent la philosophie de « la femme »

Dans deux articles précédent, nous avons proposé deux idées dont nous ferons usage dans la suite de ce chapitre. L'un sur les femmes au temps des philosophes, où il était montré que la philosophie occidentale avait besoin d'un concept comme celui de « la-femme » pour faire tenir ses jeux de contraires, et condense tout ce qui trouble l'exposé clair et transparent au réel de la philosophie, ornements, passions, etc… La philosophie classique ne peut reconnaître la femme comme autonome, elle est une fonction qui résorbe les détritus de ce que la clarté et l'ordre excluent. Les affirmations des grands philosophes sur les femmes sont à peine croyables, elles tiennent de préjugés pour une part, mais ceux-ci sont pourtant nécessaires pour fermer le système[1]. Il faut donc faire éclater les bords des contraires et construire un espace générique pour que « la-femme » soit déconstruite[2]. On comprend alors que la femme soit apparue sous un autre jour chez des empiristes anglais qui tentaient de réduire le spéculatif dans l'empirique, et donc de défaire cette circularité du système, fin 19ème, puis au 20ème siècle dans les philosophies qui ont cherché à mettre en évidence le geste de la philosophie (Jacques Derrida) ou la multiplicité des sexes (Gilles Deleuze, n-sexes).

Dans un second article, écrit avec François Laruelle[3], L'identité sexuée, nous montrions que l'adoucissement des relations entre les sexes passait par la reconnaissance de l'antériorité de l'humain (des humaines) sur le genre, ce qui est une distinction différente de celle proposée dans les études sur le genre.

Nous partirons de ces propositions comme de deux acquis,

---

1   Voir par exemple les textes réunis dans Françoise Collin, Evelyne Pisier, Eleni Varikas, *Les femmes de Platon à Derrida. Anthologie critique* (Paris: Plon, 2000).

2   « Les femmes au temps des philosophes. À propos d'une anthologie critique », *Natures, Sciences, Sociétés* 12 (2004): 204–7.

3   François Laruelle et Anne-Françoise Schmid, « L'identité sexuée », *Identities: Journal for Politics, Gender and Culture* 2, no. 2 (Winter 2003) (texte français avec une traduction en macédonien): 49–61. Réédité « Sexed Identity », *Angelaki: Journal of the Theoretical Humanities* 19, no. 2 (2014): 35–39,

1. la philosophie a besoin de « la-femme » pour faire tenir ses systèmes, et
2. l'humain(e) générique précède le genre, pour mettre en relation le genre et des critères des sciences.

Ces deux propositions ne sont pas exactement au même niveau. La plus générale est la seconde, elle marque une coupure et une irréversibilité. Elle est nécessaire pour manifester la première sur la fonction philosophique de « la-femme ». La logique philosophique est, elle, réversible, en ce sens qu'elle donne quelque considération aux textes des philosophes sur les femmes, qui ne sont dans la brillance de l'argument, viennent des fonds de tiroirs des préjugés, mais sont les déchets de la brillance et de la clarté. « La-femme » n'est jamais le centre, elle est plutôt du côté des passions que de la raison, mais elle permet de suturer le jeu des contraires philosophiques. La mise en relation de ces deux propositions nous libère des présupposés sur les différences entre hommes et femmes dans la philosophie.

Une demande méthodologique : ne pas interpréter les variables dans des continuums

De ces acquis, nous tirons une demande méthodologique : admettre des variables distinctes, mais ne pas les identifier à l'aide de continuum sociaux, historiques, culturels, philosophiques. Ne jamais interpréter une telle différence entre sexes en la focalisant sur un thème précis même si on admet la diversité des variables. Traiter ces variables sans leur donner une identité, ne plus faire de relations continues et réversibles entre différences et identités.

Laisser aller les sur-déterminations

Par conséquent, nous n'allons pas traiter la question du genre et des sciences en usant de la surdétermination de différences par d'autres, c'est-à-dire en ajoutant des propriétés que l'on voudrait féminines ou en soustrayant des propriétés que l'on voudrait masculines. Il ne s'agit pas d'admettre, par exemple, une objectivité des sciences admise et donnée des sciences classiques réputée masculine et d'y adjoindre après coup, au nom des femmes, la contextualisation, la mise en perspective, l'importance de l'émotion, le récit, la valeur éthique, la pluralité des sciences, en supposant que la première serait plutôt l'affaire des hommes et les secondes l'apport des femmes à la science. Une telle description serait contraire à notre demande de ne pas interpréter les variables à la façon philosophique, de ne pas leur donner de contenu fixe. On ne pourrait alors que déplacer des limites, exercice auquel les philosophes sont passés maîtres, mais sans les supprimer, ce qu'aucun philosophe ne sait faire.

De la même façon, la description de l'objectivité scientifique a été faite de façon trop surdéterminée elle-même dans ses relations entre théorie et faits, elle tend à exclure des pratiques que l'on pourrait très bien admettre comme scientifiques, ainsi que l'ont montré abondamment les travaux sur les modèles et la modélisation. Pour le voir, il faut revenir sur les hypothèses fondamentales de l'épistémologie. Le travail à faire est donc clair, il faut reconsidérer la question de la science, de son identité, pour pouvoir faire une place à la question du genre. Or ce n'est pas simple, car la science est silencieuse, ce sont les disciplines qui parlent pour elle. Le problème est en même temps éthique et épistémologique.

Comment l'épistémologie classique identifie la science ?

Ce qui fait classiquement le critère de scientificité est au croisement de trois séries qui se sur-déterminent, celle de l'orientation-théorie, celle de la déduction, celle de la mathématisation :

1. Celle qui va du fait à la théorie et vice-versa, qui fait que l'épistémologie classique considère leurs relations comme opposées ou complémentaires, même si bien des nuances sont apportées dans cette réciprocité, que ce soit par exemple la sous-détermination des théories par les faits par Quine, ou

encore le « Manifeste au cas où il n'y aurait pas de lois » par Baas van Fraassen.

Mais alors que faire des données, qui ne sont pas des faits, ni des corrélats de théories ?

2. Celle qui met en relation la déduction, qui est une relation d'ordre partiel, et l'implication, forme des lois scientifiques, qui est une opération de V × V dans V, V = (1,0), telle que la combinaison libre de la valeur deux propositions P et Q ait pour résultat (1011), si P = (1100) et Q = (1010). La proposition P peut être comprise comme l'une des hypothèses de la déduction et Q l'une de ses conséquences. Démontrer que de P, il est possible de déduire Q, revient à transformer P d'hypothèse de la déduction en antécédent d'une implication. Démontrer consiste à supprimer les hypothèses. On voit alors clairement que lorsque le résultat de l'implication est vrai, il y a trois possibilités (et non pas une seule), P est vrai et Q est vrai, ou alors P est faux. Si bien que l'hypothèse de la déduction ne peut être traitée de vraie, mais de supposée vraie, ainsi d'ailleurs que sa conséquence par déduction.

Mais alors que faire de la modélisation, de la simulation et des autres ingrédients de la science dont la logique n'est pas celle de l'hypothético-déductif

3. Celle qui va du plus ou moins mathématisé, du pur à l'appliqué, du fondamental au développement. Les sciences considérées comme les plus parfaites sont celles où les mathématiques sont constitutives des notions, et non réduites à traiter des données constituées sans elles.

Mais alors que faire des sciences moins mathématisées ? Sont-elles des sciences ? Les sciences doivent-elles tendre à une maturité mathématique ?

La conjonction de ces trois séries permet à la fois d'avoir une structure de la théorie et de son rapport au fait, à la fois la structure et la vérification, et aussi la robustesse des notions qui, grâce aux mathématiques, restent invariantes le long des raisonnements, et permettent d'identifier de façon plus rigoureuse ce qui est à expérimenter. Le problème majeur de cette conjonction est que toute science est évaluée entre deux bornes, celle du théorique et celle de l'expérimental, et par un critère formel, celui des mathématiques. L'effet de cette opposition ou de cette complémentarité est que les autres ingrédients de la science sont strictement interprétés dans cet espace. Cette approche de la science est évidemment très riche, elle a permis de comprendre ce qu'était un système hypothético-déductif, elle fait comprendre pourquoi un résultat d'expérience positif recouvre trois possibilités et non pas une seule comme un des ressorts les plus importants pour l'invention scientifique : il y a un X qui a presque toutes les propriétés de P, et qui n'a pas tout-à-fait celles de Q, si bien qu'il est possible de distinguer dans X deux « substances » (particules, etc…) qu'auparavant on ne distinguait pas. La distinction entre la démonstration (suppression des hypothèses en les transformant en antécédents d'implication) et la preuve expérimentale (construction d'un modèle concrétisant la théorie permettant d'isoler et de faire varier un paramètre intéressant en le mettant en rapport avec la mesure et l'observation). Quant à la mathématisation, elle permet de réduire l'hétérogénéité du réel à l'intérieur d'une discipline.

Néanmoins, par les questions posées sur les données, la modélisation, les relations entre mathématiques et sciences expérimentales, une hétérogénéité non réductible par les disciplines, on voit que l'on ne peut plus faire converger ces séries pour maîtriser une unité de la science. Chacune des séries a sa « vérité », mais locale. Il y a des morceaux de sciences qui sont théoriques, qui sont hypothético-déductifs, qui sont mathématisés, ce sont sans doute des morceaux remarquables, mais ils ne sont pas toute la science. Par hypothèse, la science postule un réel sans chercher à expliciter son rapport à lui, ce que fait au contraire la philosophie. Il n'est pas nécessaire de faire de ce que l'on a observé des théories classiques un point de vue autoritaire et excluant, il faut plutôt transformer ces distinctions de façon à ne pas fermer le concept de science sans perdre son identité.

La sous-détermination du concept de science par ses ingrédients

Cette conception classique de la science ne recouvre qu'une partie des phénomènes que l'on pourrait pourtant qualifier de scientifiques. Deux voies s'offrent à nous. Ou bien on traite ceux-ci d'éléments non scientifiques, en les considérant comme une « cuisine » sans fondement physique ou comme des échafaudages disposés à disparaître dans le résultat final. Ainsi en est-il des modèles et de la modélisation, ou encore de la simulation. Par exemple, des climato-sceptiques utilisent cet argument qui semble aller de soi et qui finalement est très agressif que la science est une alternance de théorie et d'observation, et que par conséquent il faut prendre avec précaution, voire méfiance, les nombreuses modélisations qui sont présentées autour du climat. On promeut une science 18ème siècle pour réfuter des ensembles de résultats, et la preuve c'est que lorsque l'on fait de la « bonne science », les modèles ont disparu. A ce compte, on pourrait faire disparaître toute la biologie moderne — ou bien d'autres parties de la science où les mathématiques ne jouent pas exactement le même rôle « constitutif » (Bachelard) qu'en physique. Que reste-t-il de la science ? Juste celles à partir desquelles ont été élaborés les critères cités, géométrie, mécanique, physique mathématique, physique expérimentale — à condition de faire disparaître les modèles qui ont permis de construire les conditions d'application. On pourrait reprendre beaucoup des ingrédients de la science et montrer comment ils ont été disqualifiés par cet usage. Nous pouvons prendre les exemples des concepts d'hypothèse ou de mesure. Une hypothèse est destinée à disparaître, ou bien elle est confirmée, et devient une loi expérimentale, ou elle est réfutée, et elle est abandonnée. On ne voit donc pas sa fonction, que seuls quelques très grands scientifiques avaient aperçue, Leibniz, Russell, Poincaré. La mesure est comprise comme une mise en rapport d'une série de nombres et d'une série de phénomènes, on ne voit pas les modes de précision contemporaine qui supposent la mise bord à bord de n-disciplines, et pas seulement des mathématiques et statistiques avec une série de phénomènes.

Or là, nous sommes devant un choix théorique. Ou bien nous prenons le concept science tel qu'il nous est transmis par ces lignées épistémologiques et on y ajoute des ingrédients supplémentaires par sur-détermination, ou bien l'on cherche une interprétation plus élémentaire de la science qui puisse rendre compte à la fois du classique et du non classique. Cette dernière, qui est la nôtre, consiste non plus à ajouter, mais à soustraire des hypothèses sur la science, il s'agira d'une sous-détermination et non pas de l'ajout d'une notion manquante. Cela est de conséquence pour notre sujet, parce qu'il ne s'agira pas d'ajouter à la conception des sciences classiques les « qualités » qui pourraient être celles de la femme, du type, montrons que les lois de la physique doivent être contextualisée, et pour ce faire, la femme trouvera sa place. La logique par ajout a évidemment son importance, car elle fait voir les limites d'un modèle, mais elle n'est utile que dans ce premier temps. Une fois ces limites perçues, il faut procéder autrement. Il ne suffit plus de comprendre la science comme une discipline connue prise pour paradigme + un ajout. Cela est difficile, car la discipline est le mode de visibilité des sciences, si bien que les trois critères semblent prendre une place toute naturelle. Une science « sans » discipline n'est pas immédiatement visible et elle reste silencieuse, pour reprendre un terme utilisé en un autre sens par des philosophes des sciences, Jean-Toussaint Desanti et Gilles-Gaston Granger. Elle ne signifie pas que les disciplines n'y aient plus de place, mais plutôt qu'elles ne sont plus nécessairement au centre de la création scientifique. C'est ce que nous appelons la « dérive des disciplines », ou leur « translation ».

Une épistémologie générique est justement relativement indépendante des disciplines, d'une certaine façon, elle soustrait les disciplines et, ce faisant, ouvre une espace générique, non pas au sens où ses ingrédients seraient les plus petits dénominateurs communs de celles-ci, mais dans la diversité et la richesse des concepts. Elle ne prétend pas décrire directement la science comme les épistémologies classiques, sachant qu'une telle posture conduit à privilégier un cas paradigmatique de science en fonction des champs d'étude choisis. Il nous faut une conception de la science beaucoup plus élémentaire, non immédiatement repérable sur les cas empiriques. La science est silencieuse, contrairement aux disciplines, silencieuse au sens où elle respecte une opacité du réel. Nous ne pouvons la définir que par hypothèse, comme ce qui produit des connaissances sur un X qu'elle postule mais sans développer, comme le fait la philosophie, le système des relations à ce X. De ce point de vue, une femme africaine qui observe la croissance d'une plante possède un regard scientifique, et ce qui la distingue de ceux qui font une ingénierie et une biologie de la croissance des plantes est leur volonté d'une universalité et d'une production systématisée, qui est encore autre chose qu'une volonté de science, quoi qu'en dise Aristote. C'est l'échelle qui change. Il peut y avoir de la science à toutes les échelles, c'est une question de posture plus que de langage spécialisé. Cela ne disqualifie pas les sciences spécialisées et en langage mathématique, elles combinent plusieurs sciences à la fois ainsi que des techniques. Les critères classiques ont toujours de la valeur, mais de façon locale. On peut alors les rendre indépendants les uns des autres selon les contextes et les cas. Il peut y avoir de la théorie sans fait — Quine avait déjà supposé la sous-détermination des théories par les faits. Il peut y avoir de science sans mathématiques. Il peut y avoir de la science hors la méthode hypothético-déductive –même en respectant la recherche d'hypothèses. Mais on peut articuler aussi toutes ces dimensions, en veillant bien à garder à l'esprit qu'elles sont indépendantes, et qu'elles ne vont pas nécessairement ensemble, que leur conjonction est également une création. Mais cette conjonction rend difficile l'interprétation des données, qui ne sont plus des corrélats des théories, comme le sont par construction les faits, mais ce qui fait qu'elles sont interprétées par n-disciplines ou n-théories.

Cette façon de voir la science permet de se passer par hypothèse des critères. Il y a un point où la science est réduite à une posture qui admet l'opacité d'un réel qu'elle postule. Il est possible de soustraire des hypothèses, tout en conservant la science, celle que l'on retrouve aussi bien dans les théories que dans la modélisation. La seule exigence étant que notre démarche soit à chaque pas compatible avec les connaissances fondamentales sur lesquelles les reposent. On peut, bien entendu, par hypothèse, se passer de certaines d'entre elles, mais il faudrait conserver les exigences d'hyper-compatibilité.

Dans un espace générique, les propositions provenant d'une discipline ou d'une théorie sont décomposées, de telle sorte qu'elles puissent être mises en relation avec d'autres disciplines ou théories. On peut « détacher » toute proposition de sa théorie, parce qu'elle comporte en elle l'hypothèse qui la reliait à la théorie. Si nous reprenons ce qui a été dit sur les théories hypothético-déductives, on sait que si d'une hypothèse A, on peut déduire B, alors on peut poser la proposition « A implique B ». Cette nouvelle proposition supprime une hypothèse, et peut donc être détachée de son univers théorique, on peut alors en faire usage, en se donnant des conditions de compatibilité, voire d'hyper-compatibilité, on peut construire des modèles pour un phénomène qui reposent sur des hypothèses qui peuvent être contradictoires.

On peut alors voir le raisonnement scientifique non plus seulement comme le passage d'une proposition à l'autre, mais en épaisseur, comme superposition de savoirs de disciplines différentes. Dans le cas de la déduction, il peut y avoir de la logique, des mathématiques, ou de la physique, etc. Des travaux récents sur les démonstrations mathématiques (école de Michaël Detlefsen à Notre Dame, États-Unis) ont montré cette complexité du raisonnement de déduction. Dans les régimes interdisciplinaires contemporains de la science, dans les modélisations, cette superposition est clairement engagée. Même à l'intérieur des disciplines, on peut manifester cette épaisseur et cette hétérogénéité.

De l'hétérogénéité non-standard

On peut alors traiter de science sans ajouter des propriétés à celle que l'on identifiait classiquement. Cela fait que la question du genre ne se réduit pas à la différence de l'essence de l'objectivité et d'ajouts supplémentaires qui permettraient de rajouter son contexte à la science comme étant ce qui départage le travail des hommes et celui des femmes.

Respectant notre demande de non-interprétation des différences, nous postulons une hétérogénéité aussi bien des propriétés des sujets humain(e)s et des ingrédients de la science. Ces propriétés et ces ingrédients sont des « X » qui peuvent être distribués à chaque superposition de fragments de savoirs scientifiques, en fonction de la discipline sous-déterminante qui fait « tenir » la superposition, épistémologie générique ou esthétique, par exemple.

Cette hétérogénéité est non-standard, au sens où elle ne peut être réduite par une discipline ou par un genre. Et pourtant, cette hétérogénéité ne détruit pas les différences, mais elle permet de les interpréter avec plus de douceur et de jeu. Les disciplines et les genres ne sont plus au centre, bien qu'il soit possible et même nécessaire de leur faire des emprunts, mais des emprunts eux-mêmes traités dans un espace générique.

Des « communs » entre données et faits

On sait que l'épistémologie classique organise son image de la science dans la tension entre théorie et fait, celui-ci étant le corrélat d'une hypothèse théorique. L'émergence des données, qui ne sont rattachées de façon privilégiées par aucune théorie, mais peuvent être interprétées par toutes, ont modifié cette image jusqu'à détruire l'idée de théorie, pensant que les hypothèses sortiraient elles-mêmes dans la multiplicité des données, dans une sorte d'immanence semi-empirique, ne laissant plus aucune place à une théorie indépendante, tout ce que l'on cherche étant des échantillons, des évaluations, voir des screenings plus ou moins exhaustifs. Cette image de la science qui commence à se répandre la fait disparaître dans ses propres réalisations, et elle devient tout à fait compatible avec une vision sociologique de la science, les groupes spécialisés, les échanges, devenant plus importants que les théories et les domaines d'objets. Les scientifiques seraient alors ceux qui rendraient compte des données en fonction des connaissances connues plutôt qu'en fonction du bien public.

Nous proposons une autre interprétation, épistémologique plutôt que sociologique, qui tient compte du fait qu'avec les données, les sciences expérimentales sont en train de changer de nature. Elles ne sont plus des sciences outillées par les mathématiques et l'informatique comme les classiques, elles changent fondamentalement les flux de connaissance. Cela suppose une nouvelle autonomie entre les dimensions d'une sciences expérimentale, il y a de la modélisation mathématique, il y a de l'informatique, théorique et d'ingénierie, il y a des fragments de sciences, toutes autonomes, elles ne sont réduites à des « outils ». Les sciences expérimentales ne sont plus ainsi « aspirées » par et dans les données, elles suscitent de nouveaux flux et trajectoires de connaissances, qui ne dépendent plus seulement de ce que l'on appelait théorie, mais de « pôles » distincts qui ne se confondent pas avec les données, dont il faudrait faire un équivalent de théorie. Leurs « produits » peuvent se voir alternativement comme scientifiques ou technologiques. Le mythe unificateur de la « technoscience » ne suffit plus à comprendre les sciences contemporaines.

La question n'est plus de construire une théorie, elles sont là et elles sont de toutes façons enrichies, mais de créer des « communs » ou « bien communs », à la façon d'Elinor Ostrom en économie, entre les dimensions des sciences, expérimentales ou non. Ce n'est pas une destruction des théories, elles sont là, elles s'enrichissent des avancées scientifiques, mais elles ne sont plus au centre, elles prennent un poids de garantie de compatibilité et d'hyper-compatibilité, et sont donc essentielles pour dessiner, mais de loin, comme d'un lieu géométrique, sans tenir compte de toutes les dimensions, le périmètre des sciences.

Ces communs à certains égards se forment tout seuls, au sens où ils échappent à l'ego de chaque participant. Même ceux qui travaillent de façon solitaire retrouvent dans les travaux d'autrui des problèmes et des morceaux de solutions qu'ils pensaient au départ dépendre de leur façon de les poser. Il y a une sorte d'objectivité de ces communs, qui n'est plus celle du noyau de la science. C'est l'une des formes de ce que nous avons appelé en épistémologie générique « intimité collective », chacun, chaque groupe propose des avancées et les retrouve sous d'autres formes dans le travail des autres, sans que cela se réduise à des phénomènes spéculaires. Il y a un moment où l'intimité collective transforme le sujet, au-delà de la variété des opinions. Cette intimité n'est possible qu'à dissocier l'humain(e) et le sujet, et donc à faire une autre place au genre que dans l'épistémologie classique, où les théories pouvaient encore dépendre des « ego », à la fois homme et sujet. Ce n'était pas l'homme sans qualité, mais l'homme ayant la maîtrise de la théories et de ses suites. Cette maîtrise n'est plus que locale dans les sciences contemporaines, et doit être relâchée pour comprendre la place des données et les transformations sur les sciences et les philosophies. C'est une nouvelle logique qui se met en place, plus générique qu'interdisciplinaire, mais où le générique ne se réduit pas aux plus petits communs dénominateurs, à des équivalences plates , statiques et sans orientation.

Mais il y a aussi une intimité collective de la science que l'on fabrique, celle qui donne la possibilité des trajectoires possibles dans l'espace générique, qui ne dépend d'aucune disciplines ni d'aucun ego particuliers.

Comment les communs sont-ils affectés par les genres ?
La proposition des matrices

Accepter les différences et ne pas les interpréter autour d'un thème ou d'un autre, comment faire ? Ce n'est possible qu'avec une dynamique et une orientation, que l'on peut organiser autour du concept de « matrice ». De même que la notion de « variable » s'est substituée à celle de différence, ou de jeu entre différence et identité, celle de « matrice » se substitue à celle de système. Il s'agit de sortir des complémentarités philosophiques, de ne pas répéter les chemins toujours repris en fonction de continuités données. Par la matrice, nous avons une décomposition des thèmes et des termes, mais aussi une multiplication non-commutative de leurs combinaisons. La matrice ne se réduit pas à un tableau, mais chaque « case » est elle même dynamique, produit les idées qui n'étaient pas prévues, et qui ont des effets à la fois locaux et sur l'ensemble de la dynamique. Elle permet aussi de retrouver une assise lorsqu'une idée est inventée, et de créer ainsi une solidarité à la hauteur de l'inconnu. Il y a bien des façons d'inventer une matrice, de tableau, elle devient une sphère d'idées avec une orientation, orientation objet, orientation générique,... Nous pouvons alors inventer des formes de combinaisons des ingrédients scientifiques et de propriétés de genre. Les résultats ne sont pas prévisibles, il y a une dimension aléatoire à la matrice, mais les orientations « homme » et « femme » peuvent y apparaître selon des équilibres différents, qui ne sont pas interprétables en fonction de donnés.

Ces combinaisons ont quelque chose de libérateur. Par exemple, la question de la pluralisme dans les sciences devient essentielle, celle des valeurs également. S'il y a des sciences plurielles, si les relations entre le fondamental et l'appliqué se modifient , c'est bien que la question de la valeur entre dans les sciences, ce qui était difficile dans une conception objective et autoritaire de la science. Un pluralisme encourage d'ailleurs la co-optation plutôt que de l'autorité. Il se trouve que ces thèmes ont souvent été portés par des philosophes femmes. Mais est-ce à dire qu'ils résultent des propriétés des femmes ? Ou d'un effet des communs construits dans la multiplicité des dimensions de la science ? Les sociologues pourraient bien entendu en dire quelque chose.

Mais comme philosophe, nous aimerions dire que la solution n'est pas donnée, qu'elle doit être à chaque coup reconstruite, de façon à faire des théories et des sciences un milieu où les collaborations autour des objets génériques, sortis de leurs disciplines, donnent lieu à des trajectoires inattendues, humain(e)s avant d'être une question de genre.

Reprise des deux propositions

1. « La-femme » est un mode de suture de la circularité philosophique. L'espace générique et les communs supposent que

soit ouverte cette circularité, et que, du coup, la multiplicité des philosophies apparaisse de droit. Fermer une philosophie, c'est la présenter comme le dernier « progrès », la
dernière raison de la tradition. Comment écrire en philosophie, sachant que d'autres se constituent aussi sur d'autres
hypothèses, parfois contradictoires ? On peut transposer à
la philosophie ce que Kant avait dit de la métaphysique, elle
est une mer sans rivage où le progrès ne laisse aucune trace
et sans aucun point de mire *(Les progrès de la philosophie dep-
uis Leibniz et Wolff— 1791)*. Les philosophies ne seraient-elles
alors que relatives les unes aux autres ? Si nous reprenons
les idées d'intimité collective et de commun construits dans
un espace générique des philosophies, où les concepts, sortis
de leurs logique d'origine, donnent à la fois la mesure de la
richesse de celles-ci et la possibilité de la philo-fiction, et permettent de traiter des communs inconnus, mais humain(e)
s ?

Un auteur, beaucoup cité par Deleuze, Charles Péguy, a mag-
nifiquement décrit ce problème et indiqué certains aspects de
solution :

> Une philosophie aussi n'est point une cour de justice. Il ne s'agit
> pas d'avoir raison ou d'avoir tort. C'est une marque de grande gros-
> sièreté (en philosophie), que de vouloir avoir raison : et encore plus,
> que de vouloir avoir raison contre quelqu'un. Et c'est une marque
> de la même grossièreté que d'assister à un débat de philosophie
> avec la pensée de voir un des deux adversaires avoir tort ou avoir
> raison. Contre l'autre. Parlez-moi seulement d'une philosophie qui
> est plus délibérée, comme celle de Descartes, ou plus profonde, ou
> plus attentive, ou plus pieuse. Ou plus déliée. Parlez-moi d'une phi-
> losophie sévère. Ou d'une philosophie heureuse. Parlez-moi surtout
> d'une certaine fidélité à la réalité, que je mets au-dessus de tout[4].

4   Charles Péguy, « Note sur M. Bergson et la philosophie bergsonienne », *Ca-
hiers de la Quinzaine* (avril 1914): 82–83.

Nous devons donc postuler une multiplicité de philosophies. Y a-t-il un sens à dire que certaines pourraient être plus féminines que d'autres ? Peut-être, mais, dans le débat purement philosophique, cela serait toujours repris dans les disputes spéculaires connues. Il faut que la révolte sorte du spéculaire. Imaginons plutôt des communs, philo-fictions, où la part du masculin et du féminin soit réparti aléatoirement. La fidélité à la réalité est la fidélité à l'humain(e), avant d'être celle au genre. C'est ainsi que celui-ci pourra être respecté. Et l'humain(e) lui-même philosophe par hypothèse, il n'est pas pris dans les rets de la philosophie.

2. On le voit, la première proposition nous renvoie à la seconde. On ne met pas en équivalence les philosophies sans traquer la confusion entre l'humain et le sujet. Il ne s'agit plus de faire uniquement la différence entre le sexe biologique et le genre construit, mais de faire une coupure plus radicale, entre le réel humain, celui qui vaut notre fidélité, et les sujets philosophiques, dont font partie les genres. Les sujets ont évidemment leur forme d'existence, mais s'ils sont postulés tout seuls, comme en isolation, la guerre des sexes ne peut que reprendre. Ce qui importe, c'est de conserver la force de l'hétérogénéité et de l'inconnu à la hauteur de la solidarité.

Conclusion

Nous avons proposé une mise en relation des questions de genre et d'identité des sciences en supposant qu'elle devient riche et pacifique à condition de ne pas sur-déterminer les sciences par le féminin et de revenir sur les hypothèses générales de l'épistémologie, admettant une approche épistémologique plus élémentaire des sciences. La proposition n'est pas fermée, les communs construits sont des « X » inconnus, à inventer de façon continue. La création continue des vérités éternelles, comme disait Descartes, peut-être réalisée à l'aide des deux sexes, à condition de reconnaître l'humain(e).

Notes for *And They Were Dancing*

Patricia Ticineto Clough

For Randy Martin

The composition presented below, *And They Were Dancing*, is one of five such compositions that were created over the past nine years. During this time I have been engaged in rethinking the question of the subject in terms of the ontological turn suggested by Deleuzian philosophy, speculative realism, and object-oriented ontologies, as well as feminist theories including object-oriented feminism.[1] Gaining attention in the academy in the early years of the twenty-first century, the ontological turn has encouraged a rethinking of human-centered thought in order to take up the non-human, or the agencies and animacies of objects, things, and environments. It might be thought that the turn to the non-human turns away from the human subject, the human body, human consciousness, and cognition, which cannot but raise the question: who are the subjects of this turn of thought or who became engaged with it one way or another? To raise this question does not have to mean simply reducing

1   I wrote three of the five compositions for presentation at the Society for Literature, Science, and the Arts on panels that were part of the founding of object-oriented feminism (OOF). The first panel was co-organized by Katherine Behar, Frenchy Lunning, and me. For an account of OOF, see: Katherine Behar (ed.), *Object-Oriented Feminism* (Minneapolis: University of Minnesota Press, forthcoming).

thought to the personal — biography or autobiography. Rather, it may lead us to reflect on the personal catch of arising world sensibilities, the feeling of thought stirring in a psychic arrangement, urging us to follow a subjective intuition.

There is an intuition expressed in my compositions.[2] It is that the ontological turn to the non-human has been born in part of human subjects discouraged with what thought has given, discouraged with the world not so much unchanged by thought but discouraged with the changes in the world with which thought has become, or for too long has been enmeshed. There is despair perhaps among those who most believed in the power of reason and in their power in being reasonable. Yet, in this moment of despair there also is potentiality in reason's giving way to a world sensibility, an awakening to the agencies and animacies of things, objects, and environments. Born of a felt despair and an intuited potentiality about thought itself, the ontological turn raises the question of the subject in the form of other questions: What is the representation of thought in philosophy, poetry, writing? What is the personal? What is the impersonal?

Are these questions nothing but versions of the perennial question of the woman: who is she? What does she want? This might well have been the case when *the woman* was seen to be the epistemological drive of modern thought, making it necessary for feminists to recover her, restore her, turning modern thought to her own ends — what would become part of the overdetermination of postmodernity. But it is not now that time; it is not that time, even though women still suffer, albeit differently, violence to their minds, bodies, and souls, violations of their life capacities. It is not that time; the despair and self-blaming over

2   My other compositions are: "The Object's Affect: The Rosary," in *Timing of Affect: Epistemologies, Aesthetics, Politics,* eds. Marie-Luise Angerer, Bernd Bösel, and Michaela Ott (Zurich: Diaphanes, 2014); "A Dream of Falling: Philosophy and Family Violence," in *Objects and Materials,* eds. Penny Harvey et al. (New York: Routledge, 2013); "My Mother's Scream," in *Sound, Music, Affect: Theorizing Sonic Experience,* eds. Marie Thompson and Ian Biddle (London: Bloomsbury, 2013); "Praying and Playing to the Beat of a Child's Metronome," *Subjectivity* 3, no. 40 (2010): 1–17.

the arrogance of modern thought now belongs to all of us, albeit unevenly. After all, postmodern thought demanded that everyone have their representative, so that representation of difference and identity became the aim of one wave of feminism after another, one wave of criticism after another; and we have also seen difference and identity become the currency of biopolitical governance and financial capitalism. In this context, the complaint we might raise against certain strains of the ontological turn as just more of the exclusions constitutive of modernist and postmodernist thought cannot give criticism enough psycho-political traction. For criticism to have psycho-political traction at this moment, I think it is necessary to create, to intervene quickly and steadily, to make something of what comes from thought as it sparkles before us, alluring, beautiful, enlivening, and possibly terribly dangerous. This is not just to make do, but to do, to mobilize creatively. This is my effort in the compositions I have been creating such as the one presented here.

My compositions make use of poetic expressions of childhood memory of trauma and family violence, letting them serve as commentary on current philosophy and critical theory. The poetic expressions draw on my re-experiencing of childhood memories in a psychoanalysis that I have been undertaking during the past nine years. Re-experiencing is an awkward word for conveying what happens to the subject of an analysis. This is because analysis is not so much about remembering childhood experience as much as it is experiencing with another the way objects — persons, things, environments — have become a psychic arrangement of forces and appetites, an infrastructure of (dis)attachment, repetitiously reenacted with more or less tenacity but always with some quantum of difference that is distributed unconsciously, if not non-consciously, across the arrangement. My compositions, while about trauma and family violence in the personal aesthetic of psychoanalysis, also stretch psychoanalysis to sociopolitical trauma, putting me beside myself, as I dissipate into the surrounds to become with other bodies, things, objects, environments, the stuff of poetry, making beautiful speculation about these traumatic times of violence within and without the family, the community, the nation-state, the colony, the camp. These are the times in which the philosophy and critical theory about which I write are occurring as symptom of these times or as creation against them — perhaps both.

I say beautiful not sublime, as the objects, things, and environments are not experienced as passive things; they are not only an effect of our doing. Rather, they demand something from us as if they had a liveliness of their own, a lively receptivity for a psychic arrangement. Our trauma also finds itself in the intensity of the rhythms and vibrations of these things, objects, and environments. Writing becomes a critical method that is more than representational and necessarily compositional, a matter of piecing together as a practice of allurement or enthrallment, offering a resource both of stunning clarity and tantalizing obfuscation. As such, the compositions are meant to entice those who read them, to seduce a participation in the question of the subject in the form of the other questions about philosophy, poetry writing, the personal, the impersonal of all things, human and nonhuman. To raise the question of the subject then is not to return, or to recover what has been excluded. It is to create, to compose, to intervene, to mobilize. It is to dance.

And They Were Dancing

And they were dancing:
she in a salmon colored silk gown
and he in black patent leather shoes.
They were dancing to the big band music of those times, their times.
In waves of motion, they glide past me. Gracefully,
practiced at the intricate footwork of the Peabody.
And they were dancing in those times, in time, seemingly carefree,
until a bit off beat, a tangle of feet, she slips and falls.
He goes down with her, landing on his knee.
Slow motion to dead time.
Then, suddenly
she spits words of disdain directed at him
sending a spasm of violence

through the stylish choreography of the Peabody.

My eyes shut tight.
My ears refuse to function. But something passes through:
the musical tones and the dance steps.
Sensibilities ingressing into actuality,
ghosting the present potentiality
Her afterlife and his: lingering lingering

If recently dance has captured the attention of critical theory, it is because its kinesthetic abundance not only instigates conceptual movement beyond the fixity of received categories. It also is because dance directly addresses what the body can do, and not only the human body but other bodies too — the choreographic body or object that tweaks the time of everyday movement, inviting movement to tend toward the time of the event and the experience of potential in the feel of the future in the present, when an object no longer seems to be quite what you thought it was, and the experience of time no longer feels as linear. And time slips and the choreographic objects dance:

Her silk gown thrown on the bed
and the white gardenias he gave her browning at the edge
in my head playing like a black and white movie from 1934,
before the fall, when they met in the glove factory.
He always would say that he fell in love with her immediately
hearing her sing over the din of the sewing machines.
Did he whisper: *I adore you*
in her ear, as they danced the Peabody
seemingly carefree,
in waves of motion gracefully past me?

"Events are only events because they perish." "Perishing is inevitable." Events come and perish but not into nothingness. Perished events are like memories ready for reactivation that, nonetheless invent new movement.[3] And the violence too is re-activated inventively, even more cruelly for that: the spasm of violence from them to me through the stylish choreography of the Peabody.

The spasm begins "in stillness and crescendos to extreme intensity and then dissipates."[4] But it reiterates its presence again and again unexpectedly; sometimes, its effects disappear immediately and other times they linger indefinitely, corrosive and tenacious, impregnating everything that I am resolved to grasp bringing to ruin whatever beauty there might be.

And she spits words of disdain and he to his knee again and again
The spasm of violence from them to me
I do not see.
I do not hear.
I do not know that I am there

The spasm happens from within as the body attempts to escape from itself. "It is not I who attempts to escape from my body; it is the body that attempts to escape from itself by means of…a spasm." In dance, the spasm performs the body at the edges of representation at the limits of sense as it moves into sensation.[5]

Sensations moving in both directions simultaneously
disorienting exterior and interior,
a motion that touches those who see
that touches me,
making unclear what of this spasming flesh will come to be
my body.

3   I take these words and thoughts from Erin Manning, "The Elasticity of the Almost," in *Planes of Composition,* eds. Andre Lepecki and Jenn Joy (London: Seagull Books, 2009), 117–18.

4   I take these words and thoughts from Jenn Joy, "Anatomies of Spasm," in *Planes of Composition,* 71–122. She is quoting Gilles Deleuze's *Francis Bacon: The Logic of Sensation,* trans. Daniel W. Smith (Minneapolis: University of Minnesota Press, 2002), 16.

5   Joy, "Anatomies of Spasm," from Deleuze, *Francis Bacon,* 16.

It was five years before she would agree to marry him, pitying him, she said, for having waited each and every day for her to reply. And it is as if I were there to see from the start, even before the fall, a tear in the movie from 1934. What was he waiting for? The block against love was already there, tearing apart body from psyche, tenderness from sexuality, leaving only isolated moments of release, there on the ballroom floor, leaving an excess of energy entering me bodily.

> Their dancing, like a primal scene,
> an event of violent agitation,
> a spasm agitating the flesh of their bodies enmeshed
> before I am me, if ever it is to be,
> if ever there is to be a body for me
> other than their bodies, laying there
> I should not see. I should not hear.
> I should not know what happens there.
> So near to their bed I lay,
> the fingers of my left hand tracing
> a sensing without touching,
> a dwelling in the shaping of the flowers
> made of brownish-red mahogany on the foot board of their bed.

It is said that it was to cure a spider's bite that her female ancestors from Sicily first danced the tarantella, producing a trance-like frenzy that also struck fear especially in men who should care but didn't: fathers, brothers, husbands, doctors, priests. Later they would dance the tarantella when Sicily resisted the North's imposition of the unification of Italy and throughout the massive migration at the turn of the twentieth century, the dance continued among women who were left behind or who were on their way to factories here, there and everywhere. Just as the dancing led to southern Italian women being characterized in Northern Italy as savage, superstitious or crazy, a generation later, when the women arrived in the glove factories, they often still were seen as primitive, insane, promiscuous, and racially inferior.[6]

> Was it the spider bite of history
> that made her spit poisonous disdain
> that made her female ancestors seem to others
> what she finally became:
> savage superstitious insane?

Spider (or Tarantula): It is the spirit of revenge or resentment. Its power of contagion is its venom. Its will to punish and to judge. Its weapon is the thread, the thread of morality. It preaches equality (that everyone become like it).[7]

The Peabody was danced from the early decades of the twentieth century to the years following a depression and a world war as consumerism was expanding and movies were giving ballroom dancing a wide-screened envisioning. But the dance would not be transmitted to the dancers' children. They would move to the beat of rock-and-roll in years just before the onrush of postmodernity and after dance would take itself off the dance floor and outside to the streets in hip-hop, breakdancing, and skateboarding. The unity of technique and choreography broken, dance was opened to another sociality.

If recently dance has captured critical attention, it may be for its excess energy, the in-excess of choreography. Dance no more than any other cultural practice is not simply produced by following rules. The dancing body, in "its kinesthetic specificity formulates an appeal […] to be apprehended and felt," encouraging participation and a return to the scene of dancing again and again. This is "its own version of unabsorbable excess" that comes back to the body "overwhelms the senses" as a "dreaded

6   I am drawing on the history of Southern Italian women in Jennifer Guglielmo, *Living the Revolution* (Chapel Hill: University of North Carolina Press, 2010).

7   I take these words from Gilles Deleuze on Nietzsche. See *Pure Immanence: Essay on a Life,* trans. Anne Boyman (New York: Zone Books, 2001), 94.

figure of contagion," like a devil dancing jealously, spitefully, hatefully in and around the pieces of bedroom furniture of a brownish red mahogany.[8]

> She dreamed that he would purchase them for her.
> Mirrors, chairs, dressers and the bed,
> where they lay just beyond mine,
> a cot with an iron frame
> cold to the touch
> of my fingers counting out the beats
> fingers like dancing feet.
> And I begin to wonder about the numbers in my head
> that could be orderly
> ordering the excess of energy
> made into a choreography

Only in name primal, the scene was always meant to be blinding, deafening, stupifying so that its time seems to be forever after some past pleasure, etching in flesh the very definition of pleasure as endless guilty longing for what has actually never been.

> The child left there only to see,
> hungrily, awaiting what cannot be.
> Yearning turning into the bitter haunting
> of an abstract power,
> the power of the past randomly
> to drain the potentiality of the present
> again and again, differently.
> Yet always starting with a choice,
> not made by me alone
> but also by some force

8 I take these thoughts from Randy Martin. See *Knowledge LTD* (Philadelphia: Temple University Press, 2015), 160. He is drawing on Susan Leigh Foster, *Choreographing Empathy: Kinesthesia in Performance* (London: Routledge, 2011).

of an arrangement of feet, of sheets,
of the metal frame of my bed
of my fingers tracing brownish red
feeling again for potentiality in the mahogany
feeling for the wild probabilities in a body
of artistic experimentation
for the proliferation of sensibilities
in-excess of choreography
now, more commonly realized digitally
in a program for calculating reality
but other species of actuality too
other genres of humanity.

"The program is bound up in the materialization of […] a normative field." It is "a scrim of expectation overlaid upon the real" which all the actants uphold in "a web of influence, and motivation," defending against the violation of an expressive outburst or physical act. But "the event is a violent exception or amplification, an object of fascination or concern that destabilizes a stabilized field."[9] As such, the event is also the bearer of potentiality in excess of the program, in excess of choreography.

This is dance as it assembles the gestures of actual bodies with those of virtual bodies, with virtual movements. In this sense to dance is to experiment. "Dance operates as a kind of pure experimentation" with the body's capacity to be whatever it assembles.[10]

I catch the gestures mid-flight immobilizing them in the night by means of "an ontological measuring" that nonetheless is receptive to the pressure of potentiality: "a living relationship

9   I take these thoughts and words from Jordan Crandall, "The Geospatialization of Calculative Operations: Tracking, Sensing and Megacities," *Theory Culture Society* 27, no. 6 (2010): 68–90.
10 I take these thoughts and words from Jose Gil, "Paradoxical Body," in *Planes of Composition*, 96–97.

that intermingles intensities with two extensive quantities," a mother and a father right there near my bed where I lay.[11]

I am looking back at them. Still looking back for them in the analysis of psychic memory and in a research in philosophy, studying that impossibility of fleeing in those moments when an extreme tension, a pain, a sensation of uneasiness surges toward an outside that does not exist, something that is so constituted as to make fleeing impossible while also making it necessary. It is necessary to flee this impossibility of a no outside, no elsewhere. Like the drive of sexuality, this specific excitation cannot find its discharge outside psychic memory but may never cease in its efforts to do so. To dance.

And they were dancing. In my head like in a movie from 1934, they criss-cross the ballroom floor. Their bodies facing each other, each slightly to the side of the other, they dance with some speed the intricate steps of the Peabody, indicating which steps next to take through eyes looking furtively and fingers pressing with certainty in the curve of the back or in the fold of the arm.

> Like Ginger Rogers and Fred Astair
> they were dancing gracefully
> until a bit off beat, a tangle of feet
> They fall
> They fall
> They fall together forever.

The experience of falling, falling forever, is thought to have no language and rather be a wordless bodily memory of a body being without any relation or orientation and instead being in an ongoing, near complete dissociation as profound anxiety dances free in bodily memories.[12]

11 I am drawing on the thoughts and words of Gilles Châtelet's *Figuring Space: Philosophy, Mathematics and Physics* (Berlin: Kluwer Academic Publishers, 2000), 20.

12 I take these thoughts from Donald Winnicott, "Fear of Breakdown," *International Review of Psycho-Analysis* 1 (1974): 103–7.

Yet in its backward-looking glance, the history of dance turns the error of the fall to insight about what has come to ruins and what can arise out of ruins: bodies dancing against destruction, with hope against despair, cutting through the verticality, falling to horizontality, a laterality of movement. If modern dance still is vertical while opening to the contraction, the spiral and the rapid fall to the ground, in postmodernism, there is a clearer break from the vertical, as the hinge between inside and outside is at least partially undone: dancing feet up the side of building walls and bodies flying down from high above. There is a release from being taut and vigilant. From responding in an upright position to the body's being on the floor and more, the body moves through elegant yet disjointed, unexpected articulations that call forth a reorientation of bodily spaces in relation to the forces of gravity. Traumatic drops to the knee and falling down to the ground become ordinary for bodies used to dangerous situations where risking may be the only relief. But there is more, as the body, still moving, may seize the moment where minor differences can make all the difference, where wild probabilities still prevail as forces of the real.[13]

13 I take the history of dance referenced in this last paragraph from Martin, *Knowledge LTD*, 143–212.

No: Foucault

Joan Copjec

An old accusation, resurrected by Foucault, held that Freud was a "pansexualist," that he talked too much about sex and seemed to find it everywhere. I return to this charge not to deny but, once again, to confirm it.[1] Yes, it is true that Freud discovered what we could call the *promiscuity* of sex, as long as we are clear that this promiscuity defined for him the nature of sex itself and not a moral judgment regarding an abuse of it. But if the charge of pansexualism, which aims to segregate sex, to confine it to its proper place, misses its target, it is because sex is not conceived within psychoanalysis as having a proper place, one it can claim as its own. Sexuality names not a discrete domain of life but the disjoint relation of speaking beings to their bodily existence. Isolatable neither from meaning nor biology, sex does not belong to either realm and is manifest only in the disruptions, divisions, displacements, and distortions that affect both. This basic point has a history of getting lost, going back to the time when psychoanalysis was first invented. Freud was constantly forced to parry not only the squeamish objections and outright

1   Michel Foucault, *The History of Sexuality: Volume 1,* trans. Robert Hurley (New York: Pantheon, 1978); for example, "the postulate of a general and diffuse causality [...] may well appear fantastic to us, but the principle of sex as a 'cause of any and everything' was the theoretical underside of a constant confession that had to be thorough, meticulous, and constant, and at the same time [...] scientific," 65–66.

rejections of his theory of sexuality, but also the more insidious problem of its facile, and equally squeamish, acceptance. Too often enthusiasm for his ideas relied on an effacement of their complexity and rendered them anodyne.

It is gratifying therefore to read "On the History of the Psycho-Analytic Movement," in which Freud, in high dudgeon, rises up to confront some of the most irritating sterilizations of his ideas then in circulation. He picks out for particular censure two formerly close colleagues, Adler and Jung, whom he labels, lips evidently curled, "neo-Zurich" secessionists, charging them with selecting "a few cultural overtones from the symphony of life and [...] fail[ing] to hear the mighty and primordial melody of the instincts."[2] Freud regarded these colleagues as perpetrators of a cultural plot to concoct for psychoanalysis a "family romance" in which all its major ideas of "lowly" — that is to say, sexual — origin were assigned a "higher," more elevated pedigree.

In the case of Adler, Freud focused his attack on this colleague's wildly popular notion of "masculine protest" in order to expose it as the sorry distortion of psychoanalytic thinking it was. Masculine protest is the hypothesis that both sexes recoiled from the feminine position, renouncing the passivity which that position supposedly entailed. Hopelessly confusing the "biological, social, and psychological meanings of 'masculine' and 'feminine,'" the idea of masculine protest reposed on the absurd claim that "a child, whether male or female, [c]ould found the plan of its life on an original depreciation of the female sex and take the wish to be a real man as its 'guiding line'"; and this despite overwhelming evidence to the contrary, to wit: "children have, to begin with, no idea of the *significance* of the distinction between the sexes [...] the social underestimation of women is completely foreign to them."[3] This sharp reprimand will strike

2 Sigmund Freud, "On the History of the Psycho-Analytic Movement," *The Standard Edition of the Complete Psychological Works of Sigmund Freud,* trans. and eds. James Strachey et al. (London: The Hogarth Press, 1953–1974) [henceforth, *SE*], 14: 62.

3 Ibid., 14: 55.

many of us who were too quick to understand Freud's contention — that little girls, upon noticing "the penis of a brother or
playmate, strikingly visible in large proportions, at once recognize it as the superior counterpart of their own small and incon-
spicuous organ" — as itself such a conflation.[4] Without having to
accept the problematic notion of penis envy, we can still appre-
ciate Freud's crucial point. Superficially, it seems to maintain the
innocence of children with respect to sex's significance, but the
innocence at issue is more radical: it is attributed directly to sex.
It is *sex* itself that is innocent of meaning. The corruption enters
when we try to assign meaning to it or accuse Freud of making
it the *meaning* of everything.

Adler's notion of masculine protest functioned as the ful-
crum from which the principle of pleasure was dislodged from
psychic life; it led, as Freud put it, to the complete "ejection of
sexuality from its place in mental life." The displacement of the
principle of pleasure in favor of a principle of power dispensed
precisely with the *conflictual* nature of pleasure (which is never
met with in "just measure," but always experienced, rather, as
deficient or excessive) and put forward a no less conflict-free
notion of power. Adler installed at the center of the psyche a
principle of power that took account "only of those instinctual
impulses which [were] agreeable to the [individual] and [were]
encouraged by it [...] all that [was] *opposed* to the [individual]
[...] [lay] beyond [its] horizon."[5] Eschewing the antagonistic
principles of sex and pleasure as mundane and trifling, Adler
reached for a "grander" and more "virile" principle and thus
robbed himself in the process of psychoanalysis's considerable
resources. Nothing was left for him after this initial move but to
adopt an old stand-by for thinking the contestations of power;
he ended up accepting the default notion of an abstract opposition that set the individual subject outside and against everything that was foreign and thus opposed to it.

4   Sigmund Freud, "Some Psychical Consequences of the Anatomical Distinc-
    tion between the Sexes," *SE* 19: 252.
5   Freud, "On the History of the Psycho-Analytic Movement," 14: 55.

Jung fell prey to a similar charge of family romancing. His way of dissolving the conflictual nature of sex and pleasure was to offer a monistic, de-sexualized concept of drive, one that transformed the archaic, inhuman, insistent pressure that characterized Freud's concept into an infinitely flexible and transformable theory of "interest." If wherever Freud said sex, Adler said power, wherever Freud said *libido*, Jung substituted abstract ideas that remained "mystifying and incomprehensible to wise men and fools alike."[6] The most infamous of these was no doubt the idea of archetypes, which defined an eternal, cosmological struggle between opposing terms but left each, individually, intact. If one were to convert Freud's various criticisms of Adler and Jung into a single insight, it would probably sound like this: whenever one finds two terms locked together in external opposition, you can be sure that another exorbitant term is being evaded.

If it is tempting to read Foucault's *The History of Sexuality* alongside Freud's "On the History of the Psychoanalytic Movement," it is because the former is well-situated historically to lift some of Freud's burden by detailing the way the too rapid dispersion of psychoanalysis acquired its wings from a sanitizing betrayal and distortion of its concepts. The problem, however — as everyone knows — is that Foucault had no intention of tracking this betrayal but set out, instead, to confound Freud's concepts with their aseptic reception. He had no interest in pointing out — quite the contrary — that if Victorian society was not reticent about sex, but talked about it endlessly, this did not mean that this society adopted Freud's pansexualism. Sex did not in this moment suddenly emerge as ubiquitous — or, again, as *promiscuous* — in psychoanalysis's profound sense of being irreducible to any stable point or position within the symbolic. On the contrary, all the endless discoursing about sex during the Victorian period was pressed into the service of making it over into the ideal point of the subject's cohesion, the elusive and alluring core of her identity. That this was a terrible distortion of

6   Ibid., 14: 62.

Freud's notion of sex does not dawn on Foucault, who launches into a critique of Freud's "repressive hypothesis" on the grounds that it sets up an invitation to transgressions that eventuates in the propping up of the very law they purport to transgress and tether subjects to the endless searching and safeguarding of their identities. Here is the obvious flaw in Foucault's argument: it reduces Freud's theory of sexuality—and, indeed, Freud's theory simply—to the monarchy of a single "no," *prohibition*. Not only does this leave entirely unexamined the variety of negations invoked by psychoanalysis—its multiplication of Ver-words: not only *Verdrängung* (repression), but also *Verneinung* (another term for repression), *Verleugnung* (disavowal), *Verwerfung* (foreclosure), and *Versagung* (refusal), to name the most notable—it also loses sight of the profound dimension of the unconscious. Freud knew well that prohibition is temptation and never confused it with the barrier that separated the unconscious from consciousness. The unconscious is unavailable to consciousness not because the unconscious is prohibited but because it is radically foreign to consciousness. What separates the unconscious from consciousness is not prohibition — its not being *allowed*—but something more *original*, an impossibility.[7]

"An obstacle is required," Freud wrote, "in order to heighten libido."[8] How might the Foucauldian critique of psychoanalysis parse this and numerous statements like it? We know that *The History of Sexuality* was composed as a refutation of the "often-stated theme that sex is outside of discourse and that only the removing of an obstacle, the breaking of a secret, can clear the way leading to it."[9] This refutation takes place through an inversion of the logic of that *supposedly* Freudian theme: it is not the removal of the obstacle but its emplacement that leads to what Foucault refers to as the "mirage" of sex.[10] In his argument, the

---

7   See Jacques Lacan, *Anxiety: Book X,* ed. Jacques-Alain Miller, trans. A.R. Price (Malden: Polity Press, 2014), 75.

8   Sigmund Freud, "On the Universal Tendency to Debasement in the Sphere of Love," *SE* 11: 187.

9   Foucault, *The History of Sexuality: Volume 1,* 38.

10 Ibid., 157.

obstacle is simply a lure set up by power and always in the same way, via prohibition. Far from casting sex into the shadows, power thrusts what it designates as sex under the bright lights of scientific scrutiny. Interdiction incites and proliferates discourses about sex, all of them designed to ferret it out, examine it and, in this way, perpetuate power. Saying "no" to sex, power merely increases the fascination, the frenzied obsession with it; the obstacle is thus necessary to the incitement of its own overcoming, it motivates our desire to transgress the law. Thus, it is through its supposed overcoming that the obstacle can be said to swell the tide of libido. This relation manifests itself in what Foucault describes as the "perpetual spirals of power," wherein "the pleasure that comes from exercising a power" and "the pleasure that kindles at having to evade this power" circle around and incite each other.[11] Prohibition kindles desire for evasion and sexual excitement attaches itself to the exercise of power. The "circular incitements" of this relation, the clinging harmony of their *pas de deux,* can hardly disguise the dreary monotony of the bad infinity they represent. Sex becomes an elusive ideal that perpetually recedes from grasp, and this advantages power by perpetually expanding its territory. Limits are liquidated, there is always one more step to be taken, one more turn of the spiral, but nothing really changes. Pleasure and power, pleasure and power: why only these two terms?

It has often been acknowledged that Foucault came to feel "slightly uneasy about" the argument of *The History of Sexuality,* to sense that he had "trapped himself with [his] concept of power relations" by failing to "*cross the line,*" that is, by failing to think past the impasse of a power that permitted no escape from it. He opted always for the side of power, unable to think from the other side, from "the power of the outside."[12] This trap was set, I am arguing, by Foucault's assault on negation, which ends up being far too sweeping. If the targets of his attack, Freudian

11   Ibid., 45.
12   Gilles Deleuze, *Foucault,* trans. Sean Hand (Minneapolis: Minnesota Press, 1986), 94–95.

sexuality and the juridico-discursive notion of power, go hand in hand, this is because in his understanding both only ever establish a negative connection between power and sex. And this is so, Foucault claims in a surprising moment of what looks like candor, even when psychoanalysis conceives law as *constitutive* of desire. That is, even when law is supposed to act affirmatively, it acts –in this psychoanalytic instance — negatively. Why? Because in affirming desire law prescribes it, restricts it to what it says it is; sex becomes a discursive construct; it is made into something intelligible, and it is thereby *lost*, dissolved in the vat of language. Prescription becomes, Foucault will argue, a new form of proscription.

Now, this moment of the argument is riveting for a number of reasons. First, because it arrives so belatedly in a text that has thus far seemed to ignore Lacan's contributions to psychoanalysis in favor of a vague, hearsay version of Freud that has no recourse to any actual text. Foucault's reference to the "theory of the law as constitutive of desire" sticks out because it is more accurately attributable to Lacan than any proposal vaguely attributed to Freud has been and acknowledges (minimally, inadvertently) that the position of psychoanalysis is more complex, less homogeneous than Foucault has admitted. This moment is also surprising because the position he condemns in Lacan sounds eerily similar to the one he wants to advance, the one for which he would become celebrated: power produces and affirms; it is constitutive rather than negative. We are, moreover, caught off guard by what looks at first like self-reproach. Foucault admits that it may seem that he has thus far proceeded in an "obstinately confused way...as [if he] were dealing with equivalent notions, of *repression*, and sometimes of *law*, of prohibition or censorship."[13] Here he seems to have his finger on the pulse of a problem plaguing his own argument. Yet it turns out that this is no confession, but the preface to another accusation. If he has collapsed a Freudo-Marxist notion of repression and the Lacanian notion affirmation, this is because they do not

13 Foucault, *The History of Sexuality: Volume 1*, 82.

merit distinction. "Rejection, exclusion, refusal, blockage, concealment, or mask," the differences among these various modes of negation, like the differences between Freud and Lacan are negligible since they all, ultimately accomplish the same task.[14] They all say "no" to — or post limits on — sex.

By now the repetitive nature of Foucault's reproach — that psychoanalysis relies on a juridico-discursive notion of power that operates monotonously through the single mechanism of saying "no" — has become such a lulling refrain that one almost fails to notice how much weight "saying 'no'" has accumulated, all of it negative and all of it attributed to language as such. The problem with psychoanalysis in Foucault's view is that it misconstrues *power's power as poor,* as insufficiently resourceful. "Underlying both the general theme that power represses sex and the idea that the law constitutes desire, one encounters the same putative mechanics of power," which define power in a strangely restrictive way, as "poor in resources."[15] The charge with which Foucault confronts psychoanalysis is, at base, the same as the one Freud had to confront in his battle with the Zurich school: the charge of intellectualism. But while Adler and Jung opposed Freud's intellectual *elevation* of sex, for which they preferred to substitute more worthy notions, such as power and interest, Foucault opposes the *elimination* of sex that supposedly results from psychoanalysis's appeal to language. Unlike Adler, who wanted to replace sex with power, Foucault seeks to replace language with power, this in order to turn toward rather than away from the matter of sex — in order this time to approach it as independent of language, as de-intellectualized.

On one level my observation says nothing new. Everyone knows that, unfurled, the Foucauldian banner reads, "Not language, but power." My point, however, which I will continue to push, is that Foucault's neglect of the nuances of "no" has itself been critically neglected and left unchallenged. Much of the condemnation of the juridical-discursive model of power,

14   Ibid., 83.
15   Ibid., 85.

its restriction of power to *saying* "no," invokes individual utterances. In saying "no" to something, we say it, we name it in an utterance that implants in us a desire we might not otherwise have had. Tell a child not to touch something hot and the minute your back is turned you can expect to hear a squeal of pain. Draw up a list of "thou shalt not's," ten or however many you choose, and you can be sure that they will become "the chapter and verse of our transactions at every moment of our life."[16] It is clear that interdiction is still a kind of saying. But with the mention of the Lacanian thesis that law constitutes desire, Foucault launches into an indictment of language as such and not merely individual utterances and in this case he maintains that the obverse is also true: affirmation through putting into language, *saying* as such, is also a kind of interdiction. The only difference between *prohibition*, which comes in the form of a negative utterance, and *censorship*, which is put in place by the law of desire — that is, by language as such — is that the first encourages the false hope of liberation, while the second admits the truth outright: "you are always already trapped."[17] The false hope of liberation thrives on the ruse that sexual drive is external to power, while the law of desire declares that there is nothing outside language/power. Yet Foucault suggests that this difference is not material when he reverts to the exclusive term *prohibition* shortly after distinguishing it from censorship. The law of desire is, in his consideration, a mere subset of the general "repressive hypothesis."

Let us stay with the distinction a little longer, however, to examine how it works. Foucault sets apart the *cycle* of prohibition from the *logic* of censorship. The cycle begins with his own list of commandments, seven of his own "thou shalt not's": "thou shalt not go near, thou shalt not touch, thou shalt not consume, thou shalt not experience pleasure, thou shalt not speak, thou shalt not show thyself, [...] though shalt not exist, except

16 Jacques Lacan, *The Ethics of Psychoanalysis: Seminar VII*, trans. Dennis Porter (London: Tavistock, 1992), 69.

17 Foucault, *The History of Sexuality: Volume 1*, 83.

in darkness and secrecy."[18] These commandments address themselves to the sexual drives, which are commanded to renounce themselves or else become subject to suppression. Here, there is first something — a sexual drive — that must deny itself or be forced to disappear.

The logic of censorship is different; it is simultaneous rather than sequential or cyclic. There is not something that first exists only to be forced later to disappear; rather "what is inexistent" is deprived of "the right to show itself, even in the order of speech where its inexistence is declared." [19] Foucault is not arguing that language, the order of speech, necessarily declares in an utterance the inexistence of what does not exist, nor that an utterance prohibits what is inexistent, which would be redundant in either case. He is arguing rather that language as such, conceived as the law of being, performs three operations at once. The emphasis is equally on *language, law,* and *being* and thus submits sex simultaneously to a "form of intelligibility"; a binary legislative system that distinguishes the "licit from the illicit"; and a decision as to its existence or nonexistence.[20] Foucault is charging Lacan with radicalizing Freudian negation by making it bear on existence itself and with producing thereby a triple injunction against sex. Language as such negates sex as such; it consigns sex to a "paradoxical logic" of "nonexistence, nonmanifestation, and silence."[21]

Ironically, the new historicism that launched itself in the name of Foucault embraced the idea that sexuality is a linguistic or discursive construction and ignored his primary point, the actual object of his quest, namely: "sex without law" or sex without language.[22] Sex is not, he insisted, of the order of language or intelligibility, or: reduced to intelligibility, sex is annulled. It *is* not. While psychoanalysis would agree with Foucault that sexuality is not of the order of intelligibility, it contests his concep-

18 Ibid, 84.
19 Ibid.
20 Ibid.
21 Ibid.
22 Ibid., 93.

tion of language as anemic, as "poor in resources." At the same time, insisting that there is no metalanguage, psychoanalysis also contests the characterization of language as monarchical, as a law that *dominates* the oppositions between the existent and the insistent, the licit and the illicit, the sayable and the unsayable.

The Funnel of Time and the Tide of Libido

It is fruitless to continue berating Foucault for his unapologetic conflation of forms of negation and for his characterization of language's resources as limited and limiting. Let us begin responding to his charges and discussing the way psychoanalysis views language and its relation to sexuality. We will need to restart the discussion from the place where we first spied a fork in the road, precisely in the Freudian assertion that "some obstacle is necessary to heighten libido." If we decline to follow Foucault's path by regarding the obstacle as a lure fabricated by power how then can we see it?

I attempted elsewhere to cast Foucault's interpretation of the "repressive hypothesis" into doubt by citing the Freudian distinction between the repression of ideas and the displacement of affect, but failed to develop my counterproposal very far and so I want to return to it.[23] The context from which I borrowed this distinction is significant, for the precise formulation I cited came not directly from a text by Freud but from an address by Lacan to students who were voicing discontent with their overly intellectualized, overly abstract, university education, which in the face of global issues then unfolding seemed to them anemic and irrelevant. Lacan responded that he was in a good position to answer the concerns of these students, since Freud had led the way when he was obliged, in his day, to answer to similar complaints about the "'intellectualization' of the

23 See my essay, "The Sexual Compact," *Angelaki* 17, no. 2, special issue on "Sexual Difference between Psychoanalysis and Vitalism" (June 2012): 31–48.

analytic process, on the one hand, and the maintenance of the repressed, on the other."[24] Lacan goes on to argue that Freud's response — which grounded itself on its formulation of the concept of negation (*Verneinung*) — is what ultimately gave psychoanalysis the weight it needed to stand up to the misgivings concerning its consequentiality, that is, its real world effectiveness. It is the reference to negation that introduces and accounts for the distinction I mentioned a moment ago: although ideas can be repressed, "Freud explicitly stated that [...] affect is [not] repressed [...]. [A]ffect [...] is effectively displaced, unidentified, broken off from its roots — it eludes us."[25]

Because it is pivotal for the claim that the resources of language and psychoanalysis are more robust than Foucault warrants, and enable them to intervene in the world, we will want to take a detailed look at the concept of *Verneinung*. But before we do, a couple of preliminary remarks will help flag and thus hold firmly in mind the stakes involved.

1. That the absence of any mention of affect from Foucault's account of sexuality did not ignite outrage or even mild surprise in readers only confirms the message Lacan was attempting to get across: those who were blinded by his emphasis of the linguistic dimension of psychoanalysis from seeing there any evidence of affect were surely laboring under a distorted notion of affect as independent of language. For Freud and Lacan, affect is unapproachable except via language. This means that the direct access to bodies and pleasures Foucault hoped to achieve could only remain a pre-critical pipe dream; for by setting out to bypass language, one loses affect — which is sited in the body — in the bargain.

24 Jacques Lacan, "Response to Jean Hyppolite's Commentary on Freud's Verneinung," *Ecrits*, trans. Bruce Fink (New York and London: W.W. Norton, 2006), 322.
25 Jacques Lacan, *The Other Side of Psychoanalysis: Book XVII*, ed. Jacques Alain-Miller, trans. Russell Grigg (New York and London: W.W. Norton, 2007), 144.

2. The impasse in which Foucault found himself makes plain the roadblocks we have to clear. The problem, as mentioned (and not only by us), was his inability to conceive an outside of power even as he accused psychoanalysis of the same crime by tethering every resistance to the short leash of law. In the juridico-discursive model, so says Foucault, power just *is* this tethering of outside to inside, *is* the very guarantee of their articulation; every resistance remains under the jurisdiction of power. Opposing this model, Foucault sees no other way out than to deny power an *inside*. Since power, in its productive rather than negative capacity, is endlessly ramifying, without boundaries, we need not fear the prison doors of power closing around us.

The way in which Foucault declares his position on this score is memorable: "On needs to be nominalistic, no doubt."[26] With this he rejects, as nominalists do, all universals, every all-embracing institution and structure, insisting rather that although the myriad of specific, local, and capillary *techniques* may be integrated or consolidated these processes of coagulation are always only secondary and unstable. But nominalism is not just a rejection of universals; it is also a conception of language that wants to reduce it to its denotative function. It believes language sticks names on things. In the hands of an oppressive power, language can be diverted from its proper function of naming actual things to name things that had no actual existence. If nominalism was once considered a radical position, this is because historically it performed the role of demystification, denouncing entities such as the Church and the infallible authority of the Pope as baseless fictions. Believing that language is irreducible to its denotative function and that universals are not so easily dismissed, Lacan rejected the "danger of idealism" lurking in the nominalist tradition outright. "I am not a nominalist," he declared, for it is not

26 Foucault, *The History of Sexuality: Volume 1*, 93.

the case that "the symbolic system is [...] like a piece of clothing which sticks to things."[27]

The History of Sexuality regards language as a sovereign power ruling over its own sovereign acts of division between existence and inexistence, the licit and illicit, the sayable and the non-sayable. We can make a preliminary approach to the contrary view of language held by Lacan by taking a look at his discussion of a sign in the *Encore* seminar. There he insists that smoke "always is" the sign of a smoker; there is "no smoke that is not the sign of a smoker." Strange, because according to the common saying, smoke is the sign of fire. What point is Lacan trying to make by substituting the smoker for the fire? In the strict sense, a sign is correlated with a presence outside language, that is, with something that denotes an exterior. But Lacan alters the strict sense to claim that smoke is "not the sign of something, but of an effect [which] is [supposed] as such by the functioning of the signifier."[28] It is evident that he is redefining signs here less in opposition to signifiers (which function in relation to other signifiers rather than to something outside) than as a special effect of them. A sign is a signifier whose "meaning effect" has been suspended, but which has this other "special effect," as I am calling it, not of denoting a presence but of "supposing" it. Lacan has often spoken of the subject as "supposed" by the signifier; here it is again a question not of something but of someone (a subject) who is supposed. The smoke, observed on a deserted island, is taken as a sign that there is someone else present, "another man." Yet this supposition can no longer be understood according to the logic of denotation since it is associated, as we said, with this new function, which suspends meaning. We should think then of this other presence as spectral, not in the sense of a mere illusion but in the sense in which

27 Jacques Lacan, *Freud's Papers on Technique: Book I,* ed. Jacques-alain Miller, trans. John Forrester (New York and London: Norton, 1988), 265; and Jacques Lacan, *Le séminaire XVI. D'un autre à l'Autre* (Paris: Seuil, 2006), 28.

28 Jacques Lacan, *Encore: On Feminine Sexuality and the Limits of Love and Knowledge: Book XX,* ed. Jacques Alain-Miller, trans. Bruce Fink (New York and London: Norton, 1998), 49; translation altered.

Marx thought spectrality: as something produced but not contained by the system. Lacan is arguing that language produces an outside that it does not dominate. How should we think of this spectral outside? As a disturbance of the solitariness of our existence, a surplus that calls into question our solitary and sovereign perspective on the world. The sign, and thus the implication of another presence is "capable," Lacan says, "of arousing desire."[29] And as desire is, for Lacan, always primarily desire of the other, we can begin to see that this question of the sign bears on the subject's relation to the other rather than her sovereignty.

As it turns out, it is precisely in the direction of relation that Foucault wants to take his defined notion of power, which he wants to put in the place of language. Power is omnipresent not because it issues from a central, sovereign point, he maintains, "but because it is produced from one point to the next, [...] in every *relation* from one point to another."[30] Foucault dons the nominalist mantle in order to substitute relations among a multiplicity of strategies for universals that might otherwise overhang and distribute them. The difficulty is that relations are for him a solution without first being a problem. Foucault never problematizes, never attempts to provide a *theory* of relations, which are not one of the strategies or things related, but something other. Do things precede relations or do relations precede the things they relate? If nominalism asserts that there are only things in their particularity, how does it account for relations?

Lacan, on the other hand, is well known for his problematization of relation and for inaugurating his conceptualization of it in a negative manifesto, "There is no sexual relation." It is the universality of this negation, which forbids the unification or fusion of man and woman into an all, a positive universal, that is the condition of the possibility of sexual relations. This is not the place to pursue this argument further, but it should draw attention to the fact that *relation* is a dormant term in Foucault; it is a simply non-functional. If the assurance he offers — namely

29 Ibid., 50.
30 Foucault, *The History of Sexuality: Volume 1,* 93.

that while power comes from everywhere, it does not embrace everything — rings hollow, it is because we soon realize that his ramifying notion of power as being without boundaries, barriers, or doors is also without exits. The difference between the "pansexualism" of psychoanalysis and Foucault's insistence that "power comes from everywhere" lies precisely here with their conception, in the first case, lack of any conception, in the second, of the boundaries or limits that allow relations to be forged.

From this point we can turn back to the concept of *Verneinung*. While Foucault acknowledges that there is a more radical form of negation than prohibition, the one with which he chiefly deals, he attributes the radical form to Lacan, without acknowledging that Lacan based his position on the radical concept of negation developed by Freud in his brilliant essay, "Negation."[31] This is, as we said, the concept on which Lacan relied to refute the charge of intellectualism with which Foucault tried to tar psychoanalysis. This charge was not only not new, it plagued Freud in his day, but was enjoying a new vogue in Paris at the time Foucault wrote. *Verneinung* is not subject to the dynamic force of repression that enables the famous "return of the repressed" to consciousness and bears less on a particular prohibited act or object than on reality itself. If, indeed, this fact is alluded to by Foucault, it is badly caricaturized by his claim that Lacan's constitutive notion of law "denies existence" to particular acts or objects. "Denies" is weak. Foucault intends it to be. He prefers to underestimate the boldness of the Freudian hypothesis, which posits that there is from the very beginning a primal *deduction,* a radical expulsion of reality by language. Psychic life does not simply suffer this loss, it is founded on it; from here on out "nothing exists except against a supposed background of absence."[32] From the moment she is born, the subject is denaturalized and objects no longer appear to her in their immediacy.

31 See Michel Foucault, "The Mesh of Power" (1976), *Viewpoint Magazine,* Sept. 12, 2012, https://viewpointmag.com/2012/09/12/the-mesh-of-power/.
32 Lacan, "Response to Hyppolite," 327.

This thesis is manifest in various ways in Freud, but we see it most clearly in his positing of one primary lost object: the mother, or das Ding, the Thing, as Freud refers to it in *Project for a Scientific Psychology* (1895). The prohibition of incest operates in psychoanalysis at this level of irrecoverable loss. Prohibition is therefore unfortunate in terms of the argument Freud develops, for it invites confusion with its false friend, *prohibition*, as in saying "no" to or forbidding something, as in all the "thou shalt not's" of the commandments, whether the Biblical ten or the Foucauldian seven. Foucault clearly falls prey to this confusion when he speaks about incest in *The History of Psychoanalysis*, for he makes its so-called "prohibition" the paragon of prohibition, the nay-saying "rule of rules" occupying the threshold of all cultures, societies, and individuals.[33] In reality, he contests, this prohibition functions merely to consolidate a particular historical form, the bourgeois family, which emerged at a specific moment as a hot-bed of forbidden desires, which family members were incited to examine and confess. "By devoting so much effort to [...] the transcultural theory of incest, anthropology [...] proved worthy of the whole modern deployment of sexuality."[34] The reference to anthropology is designed to ring the bell of truth, immediately to call to mind Lévi-Strauss and the complaints against structuralism then being voiced. Lévi-Strauss secured his structural anthropology, Foucault intimates, less on the study of particular cultures than on a supposedly universal but in reality quite parochial claim that culture as such is founded on the taboo against incest.

Foucault does not mention the fact that the psychoanalytic concept of the incest taboo differs from Lévi-Strauss's, which bears primarily on the relation between fathers and daughters, on the admonition against the hoarding of women. By way of separating culture from nature, accounting for the emergence of culture, Freud focuses, rather, on the son's incestuous desire for the mother, but nowhere claims that this desire follows from a

33 Foucault, *The History of Sexuality: Volume 1*, 109.
34 Ibid., 109–10.

prohibition of the mother. Not even in the ten commandments is it specified, Lacan points out, "that one must not sleep with one's mother."[35] The prohibitions enunciated in the commandments are part and parcel of culture itself, which is evident in the fact that they are broken daily. What is at work in the founding of culture is something stronger than a prohibition of the mother. The mother, or a dimension of her, is quite simply deducted, subtracted; that is, the natural relation or relation to nature she implies is lost to speaking beings. Thus, contrary to Foucault's complaint that the repressive hypothesis attains its highest form in the incest taboo, which sets itself up as the unvarying law of all cultures and restricts the forms it may take, Freud's deduction hypothesis subtracts the natural ground of cultures, the universal good union with the mother-who-gave-birth-to-you implies. Rather than restrict the form cultures may take, this subtraction makes it impossible to posit a necessary relation between nature and culture. It cuts the link between them.

Yet there is no avoiding the fact that this last statement can appear to run into a different kind of trouble; it can seem to court idealism. This is where a fuller discussion of *Verneinung* must begin. To student grumblings about the ineffectiveness of mere intellection and Foucault's charge that psychoanalysis inscribes sex in an order that "operates [...] as a form of [mere] intelligibility," *Verneinung* remains prepared to give an answer, even as it gives the opposite impression. A crucial point of Freud's essay is that even if analysis sometimes succeeds "in bringing about a full intellectual acceptance of the repressed [by the patient]; [...] the repressive process itself [will] not [be] [...] removed."[36] Now, is this ineffectiveness of the "intellectual acceptance" brought forth by analysis not the very criticism (as per Lacan's claim, quoted earlier) against which psychoanalysis had

---

35 Lacan, *Ethics*, 69.

36 Sigmund Freud, "Negation," SE 19: 236. My reading of Freud's essay relies on the superb, classic readings by Hyppolite and Lacan (cited above) and the equally excellent recent reading by Alenka Zupančič, "Not-Mother: On Freud's *Verneinung*," *e-flux* 33 (March 2012), http://www.e-flux.com/journal/33/68292/not-mother-on-freud-s-verneinung/.

to defend itself? Does not this failure to remove the repression condemn psychoanalysis for putting too much stock in its poor resource, language? At the opening of the essay, "Negation," a patient blurts out the following, "You ask who this person in the dream can be. It's *not* my mother." But, Freud continues, "We emend this to: 'So it *is* his mother.' In our interpretation, we take the liberty of disregarding the negation."[37] This little *ur*-scene of psychoanalysis seems to set it up as the butt of jokes: not only is psychoanalytic interpretation lacking in effectiveness, it also appears to be arbitrary, even despotic in the "liberties" it takes. Let us take care, however, for precipitous criticism will fail miserably here.

The fact that the patient's repression is not eliminated, but persists, does not invalidate Freud's insistence that the analyst is somehow *licensed* to count the patient's negation as affirmation. On what grounds? Because psychoanalysis does not conceive repression as entirely reducible, it does not seek simply to abolish it; the point of psychoanalysis lies elsewhere. As we have noted, we pay a ransom for our access to language; something is deducted, permanently, from what can be said. It is as if something were, from the beginning, subtracted from existence; as if every speaking subject were subject to a pure or lost past that was never present, never experienced. To this extent, we can agree with Foucault when he insists, in his charge against psychoanalysis, that language does not simply affirm, make intelligible, but also negates, casts "into oblivion, [into] inexistence"; language, it is true, "denies existence." For this very reason the analyst who reads her patient's negation as affirmation does not demonstrate pure arbitrariness, our capacity to say whatever we please — you say "no"; I say "yes" — as if nothing more were at stake. Counting the patient's negation as affirmation, the analyst acknowledges, rather, that there is something that does not serve at our pleasure and that this has undeniable consequences for understanding psychic functioning. The patient's blurted out denial, "It's not my mother," negates a prior negation, the

37 Freud, "Negation," 19: 235.

one that surrenders the mother, as *das Ding,* to inexistence, to an irretrievable, primordially lost past. Eurydice-like, she will forever remain behind, repressed, in the strongest sense. The patient's denial does not negate that negation or primordial repression; it does not *lift* the repression, in this sense. The mother remains under the pall of repression, inexistent. And yet, in proper Hegelian fashion, the negation of the negation is not for nought. For, by means of the symbol of negation, something is *affirmed,* accepted; the Freudian concept of *Bejahung* (primal affirmation) means just this: the symbol (of negation) affirms (the negation that is) primary repression, that is to say, it affirms the existence of the unconscious as such.

Freud's argument regarding the effectiveness or resourcefulness of language does not yet address, however, Foucault's full charge that language, which governs the order of intelligibility only, excludes or is antithetical, by its very nature, to the order of bodies and pleasures, that is, to sexuality. At first glance, Freud appears to confirm this accusation when, immediately after admitting that the patient's negation of the idea that his dream was about his mother does not bring an acceptance of what's repressed, he states simply, "We can see how in this the intellectual function is separated from the affective process."[38] In his commentary on Freud's essay, Jean Hyppolite warns that that it would be a "gross oversight" to take Freud at his word here, for in fact, in carrying out his analysis of the intellectual function, "he does not show how the intellectual separates from the affective, but how the intellectual is [a] sort of suspension of content."[39] Responding to this commentary, Lacan seconds Hyppolite's contention that the affective "preserves its effects" through the intellectual rather than being separated from it. If this point is obscured it is because "backers of the new psychoanalysis" make the mistake of conceiving the affective as "a psychological *qualitas occulta* to designate that 'lived experience' whose subtle gold,

38   Ibid., 19: 236.
39   Jean Hyppolite, "A Spoken Commentary on Freud's 'Verneinung,'" in Lacan, *Ecrits,* 748.

they claim, is only rendered through the decanting of a high alchemy."[40] It would be hard to miss how closely Lacan's mocking tone and vocabulary mimic Freud's dismissal of the "Zurich secessionists" for their inability to conceive the link between the intellectual and the sexual.

The 1924 essay, "Negation," is a compressed "critique of judgment" that carries through the insight Freud first sketched in the "Project," namely that intellectual judgment is tied to *das Ding,* the never experienced object of a primordial pleasure. That is, Freud was from the start intent on articulating a link between pleasure and intellect, not their absolute separation. "Negation" describes the emergence of judgment as unfolding in two stages. While he at times began from the premise that there was first a hallucinatory interiority that was later breached, or opened to an outside, here he asserts that the beginning is marked by a division, created by the ego's taking into itself what is pleasurable and spitting out or expelling what is unpleasurable. Judgment proper only begins at a second stage that seems at first to reinforce this division by affirming or negating the existence of what is pleasurable, on the one hand, unpleasurable on the other. But in fact the second process is not as symmetrical to the first as it looks at first. For, as Hyppolite keenly observes, affirmation is described by Freud as a *substitute* (*Ersatz*) for the ego's "taking in" or "uniting with" presentations, while negation is said to be a successor to or consequence (*Nachfolge*) of the ego's expulsions.[41]

What is the significance of this asymmetry? The quickest way to answer is to say that the psyche is shown *not to be dominated by opposing forces of affirmation and negation.* Foucault's claim that psychoanalysis submits sex to a binary system that separates the licit and illicit, the intelligibility of what it calls sex and the unintelligibility of actual bodies and pleasures is invalidated by Freud's introduction of a third term that brakes these compulsive oppositions. Listen to the way Freud says this: "the

---

40 Lacan, "Response to Hyppolite," 320.
41 Hyppolite, "A Spoken Commentary on Freud's 'Verneinung,'" 752.

symbol of negation [...] endow[s] thinking with a first measure of freedom freedom from the consequences of repression and, with it, from the compulsion of the pleasure principle."[42] Freud had begun making this argument a couple of years earlier in "The Ego and the Id," where he wrote about a "resistance to the compulsion [of a repressed drive], a hold-up in the discharge reaction" that allowed "'something' [...] [to] become conscious as unpleasure."[43] Rather than compulsively spitting out, attempting to destroy, all that is non-recognizable and therefore unpleasurable, the ego, through the intervention of the intellectual symbol of negation, allows "something" unpleasurable to come to consciousness.

The quotation marks indicate that what comes to consciousness is nevertheless held at a distance from it. This is because we becomes conscious not of an idea, but precisely of an affect, which had formerly been unconscious. Yet even as conscious, *affects remain foreign to consciousness,* which is unable to transcend them. This means that all affects are in some sense unpleasurable in that their alterity disturbs the ego, which is unsettled by the awareness of a larger economy than the one over which it purports to rule. This unpleasure is what *shoves* thinking forward or, as Freud puts it, "decides the choice of motor action, which puts an end to [...] postponement [...] and [...] leads over from thinking to action."[44] At this point we are able to discern a non-Foucauldian reading of the psychoanalytic dictum that "some obstacle is necessary to swell the tide of libido," for the symbol of negation resists or, puts up an obstacle to the appetite for destruction, gives rise to affect (or, in the vocabulary of "The Ego and the Id," to the emergence of unrepressed id). The symbol of negation reaches back, sending the subject through a "temporal funnel," as it were, to the never experienced

42 Freud, "Negation," 19: 239.
43 Sigmund Freud, "The Ego and the Id," SE 19: 22.
44 Freud, "Negation," 19: 238.

Thing, the pure past of *das Ding,* and remembers it forward, "re-finds it" in the very disorientation of affect.[45]

I cited earlier Hyppolite's hypothesis that despite what Freud says, he does not in fact separate the intellectual from the affective, but demonstrates rather that the intellect has the power to suspend content. I stopped short, however, of citing the hypothesis fully, lest it provide fodder to complaints against psychoanalysis's intellectualism. Hyppolite goes on to say that it would "not be inappropriate" to use a "somewhat barbaric term" for the relation Freud establishes between intellect and affect, namely sublimation.[46] According to the common reading, sublimation is a kind of "high alchemy" by which raw sexuality is transmuted into some refined, de-sexualized form. In this context, however, we suddenly see that rather than efface or replace libido with something less libidinous, *sublimation is that process which gives us access — through the intervention of the symbolic — to libido.* Simply put, *we would have no affects without symbolization.* We also see, at the same time, that affect — bodies and their pleasures — are not available to us as immediate "lived experience," but rather as an experience of the unlived. That which does not exist for the subject, non-being, is converted by the symbol of negation to an experience of radical otherness. The concept of affect that emerges in Freud is certainly not that of an immediacy at which we could arrive by leaping out of language. Affect is, rather, the phenomenon of an exposure from within and by means of language to what is outside it.

I cannot claim really to know what Foucault is looking for at the end of *The History of Sexuality* when he calls for a different concept of bodies and their pleasures, but I suspect that this *qualitas occulta* is nowhere to be found.

---

45 I borrow this term from Lacan who invents it his discussion of the Wolf Man case, "Response to Hyppolite," 326.

46 Hyppolite, "A Spoken Commentary on Freud's 'Verneinung,'" 748.

Thinking WithOut

Jelisaveta Blagojević

Although words such as feminism, gender, women are not included in the title, and are hardly mentioned in the whole
text — they are at the very heart of it. It is only through feminist
theory that I have realized what it means to have a non-smug
theory that is not all about self-satisfaction, self-promotion, and
self-preservation as is the case with most Western theoretical
projects; it is only through feminist politics that I have discovered what it means to have politics that is not translated into the
preservation of the status quo and/or reduced to an instrument
of power.

Generations of feminists are showing us how being political always calls for one's own undoing; it involves re-imagining
and re-inventing our own positions, locations, and belongings.
And finally, it is a life of experiencing the invisibility of women's
thinking and doing that teaches us — if we want to make a difference, if we are looking for a change — not to rely on what is
visible, thinkable, sayable, audible, or generally, on what is given
or taken for granted.

1. The Art of Voluntary Insubordination

The question "What, therefore, am I, I who belong to this humanity," the one that Foucault poses in "What is Critique," indicates the rethinking of the present and involves the necessary

radicalism of the practicing critique[1]: It asks what's going on just now? What is happening to us? What is this world, this period, this precise moment in which we are living? All these questions account for ways of rethinking the present, which does not allow us to posit ourselves outside of the possible answers. There is no epistemologically, ethically, ontologically, and politically pure or neutral ground to ask any kind of critical question without being desubjugated and thus self-transformed by that very gesture.

A critique does not consist in merely making a value judgment in accordance with criteria or ideals already in place, that is, saying that things aren't good the way they are. It would be too simple. It is more about looking into various assumptions, familiar notions, established and unexamined ways of thinking upon which the accepted practices of our time are based. Critique, in these terms, would necessarily involve being — untimely, out of synchronicity, while speaking from a position anchored in the present and its regulating conditions. Thus, to do criticism means to make it harder to be governed, as Foucault would say. To do criticism involves the "art of not being governed or better, the art of not being governed like that and at that cost — or the art of not being governed quite so much."[2] It means not accepting as true what an authority tells us is true, or at least not accepting it because an authority tells us that it is true.

Foucault's distinction between government and governmentality points to the ways how the apparatus denoted by the former enters into the practices of everyday life of those who are being governed — how it enters in our very ways of thinking, doing, and being. To be governed is not only to have a form imposed upon one's existence, but to be given the terms within which existence will and will not be possible. Therefrom, the no-

---

1   Michel Foucault, "What is Critique?," trans. Lysa Hochroth, in *The Politics of Truth*, eds. Sylvère Lotringer and Lysa Hochroth (New York: Semiotext(e), 1997), 41–81.

2   Ibid., 28–29.

tion of critique demands, requires, calls for self-transformative practices.

If the I who is thinking is not endangered, destabilized, shaken, undone by the process of thinking itself — such way of thinking one could not call a critique at all. And it is precisely this self-transformation that makes every step that we take being possibly the invention of the unthinkable. Critique, or "the art of voluntary insubordination,"[3] as Foucault would call it, has to insure the desubjugation of the subject in the context of the politics of truth. Therefore, insubordination to the political conditions of the present demands the insubordination of one to oneself.

There is no possibility of non-demagogical thinking, thinking which merely preserves the status quo and as such is an instrument of power — within the field of thinkable, sayable, visible, or audible — or generally — within the field of what is given and taken for granted.

2. Non-Thought

The thought, if we are to pursue the Foucauldian notion of critique, pushes toward the direction of non-thought, but that non-thought is "not external to thought but lies at its very heart, as that impossibility of thinking."[4] Non-thought is thus a condition of thinking precisely because it cannot be thought, yet it simultaneously represents that which calls for and demands thinking.

Allow me to make a digression now:

On the various internet sites where Woody Allen's quotes are listed, one of the most popular one says: "I believe there is something out there watching us. Unfortunately, it's the government." What makes us laugh in this statement of Allen's can probably be rephrased like this: you, funny people, you believe there is a

3 Ibid., 32.
4 Gilles Deleuze, *Foucault*, trans. Séan Hand (Minneapolis: University of Minnesota Press, 1988), 97.

God somewhere out there watching and protecting you, but it is much more trivial and obvious — it is only the government, the disciplinary mechanisms of power and its micro-physics.

Unfortunately, however, Allen is aiming to reveal the crude truth about the fact of who or what is settling our "outside" — the point that we can make about the world that we live in is much more scary: *there is no outside at all.* We live in a world in which the "outside" as a possible horizon of the change has been hijacked and stolen. As a result, today, almost everything appears equally thinkable — the sufferings, horrors, and tortures, the end of the life on Earth, market-oriented everyday life, proprietary structures in capitalism, the militarization of the world, etc.

It appears that the problem of the relation between thinking and politics is not only, as we used to think, that the inner logic of thinking preserves the absolute privilege of the existing dominant social order (by not questioning it) and its normative aspects by rendering unthinkable, and thus by casting outside the political domain, the possibility of a resistance to this "unquestionable" organizing principles of social relations, some of them being family, nation, religion, but also patriarchy, heteronormativity, etc. What late capitalism has produced is the claustrophobic maneuver of positing that everything is always already included, calculated, possible, thinkable: so, what it took from us is precisely the notion of the "outside" that has been, for a long time, linked to the domain of madness, to the domain of literature, or to that of revolution. We live today in the world without outside and we are thinking without an "outside." On the other hand, in order for thinking not to be a mere repetition of the already known as an "unquestionable" organizing principle of social relations, it has to be the thought of the outside, it has to come from the outside, to stretch in relation to the outside, to be towards the outside, belonging to the outside.

In his book on Foucault, Deleuze has pointed to several crucial aspects in relation to the question of Foucault's "Thought of the Outside," and his efforts to search for the ways it would be possible to think otherwise: first, the task of thought is to liberate the forces that come from the outside; secondly, the outside is always an openness to a future; ("In this way the outside is always an opening on to a future: nothing ends, since nothing has begun, but everything is transformed"[5]); the thought of the outside is a thought of resistance (to a state of affairs); and finally, the force of the outside is Life.[6]

Thought demands from us to make fiction a necessity and to fictionalize order's unquestioned status of being reality, to invent new relationships, new possibilities of being-together, solidarity and sharing, that is, modes of being-in-common outside the sentimentalized logic of protection, and the mirroring and self-reflective narcissistic claims of identity. It demands, I would argue, thinking and enacting modes and practices of communality which would be capable of engaging us in order to question power regimes as such and open futurity towards differences not yet anticipated in the normalized frames of present political horizons.

To think is obviously to think "something," but at the same time to think the specific place where this thinking occurs. Those who think are necessarily put into question by the very act of thinking. Those who think are the double folded side of the object of their thought. If this is not the case (if there is no response to this political, ethical and epistemological call to think oneself thinking), thinking is reduced to a peaceful pace, to the "pre-given," to that "something" being demogogically offered to thinking — the thought of the familiar. Thinking understood in this demagogical way means to be assigned to think, expected to think, demanded to think — properly — in accordance to the law, to the imperative of common thinking. This imperative states: don't just think, but think properly — and, we might add, think normatively, be obedient in thinking.

In line with Foucault's notion of *pensée du dehors*, we can surely state that there is no *proper side of thinking*, some determining criteria that would guarantee us that we are thinking properly. Thinking implies wanderings and deflections, de-

5   Ibid., 89.
6   See ibid., 89–95.

tours — thinking is always seductive. It is not on the "right path," it can never be. It is misleading, and involves demanding task of turning from the "right path," from the political and ideological pattern that gave birth to the normative notion of the "proper" side of thinking, or of the practice of taking sides in thinking, of "sides" as such.

As Foucault argues:

> It [critique] must be an instrument for those who fight, resist, and who no longer want what is. It must be used in processes of conflict, confrontation and resistance attempts. It must not be the law of the law. It is not a stage in a program. It is a challenge to the status quo.[7]

Accordingly, critique would always mean a certain re-composition, an invention. It means that being political today demands from us an effort of re-imagining, re-inventing our thinking and doing, as well as rethinking the limits and possibilities within which our existence will and/or will not be possible.

3. I Don't Say the Things I Say Because They Are What I Think

At the very end of his interview for Dutch TV — which, as the story goes, was lost — Michel Foucault (with his mystical, seductive smile) says: "I don't say the things I say because they are what I think, I say them as a way to make sure they no longer are what I think."[8]

One of the possible ways to understand this seemingly non-logical, puzzling, and paradoxical statement follows the certain tradition of thinking in the history of the so-called "Western" philosophy in which thinking is understood as something that

---

7   Michel Foucault, "Table ronde du 20 mai 1978," in *Michel Foucault: Dits et écrits II, 1976–1988* (Paris: Gallimard, 2001).

8   An interview which was made with Foucault by Dutch philosopher Fons Elders was preceded by discussion "Human Nature — Justice versus Power" between Foucault and Chomsky on Dutch TV in 1971. The interview was published in Michel Foucault, *Freedom and Knowledge,* eds. Fons Elders and Lionel Claris (Amsterdam: Elders Special Production BV, 2013), 25–47.

cannot be "objective." Should it be assumed that one of the aims of thinking is the achievement of a certain kind of comprehension, a holistic, stable, and coherent thought intending the object of thinking — as we already said, that very thought will necessarily encompass the one who is thinking, which might, furthermore, cause a specific vertigo in which the thinker and the object of thought are integrally intertwined.

Foucault's sentence "I don't say the things I say because they are what I think, I say them as a way to make sure they no longer are what I think" seems to imply that when we are thinking, we never think what we actually think we think, but instead we are caught in this endless, dizzying shifting of thinking and non-thinking, between thinker and the object of thought. This oscillation occurs in a manner which indisputably — for even the tiniest interval or moment in time — excludes the possibility of identification, stabilization, or determination of the positions (between the one who thinks and what is thought) — except in their eternal and dizzying shifts and exchanges.

This Nietzschean view of knowledge as a product, result, and effect of power struggles, that Foucault adopts, has important consequences for the understanding of the "subject" of knowledge. Foucault does not understand the subject as universal, timeless or abstract, as being the source of how one makes sense of the world, and the foundation of all knowledge, thought and action. For Foucault, the knowing subject, the one traditional epistemology speaks about, does not exist in his/her autonomy and universality. Foucault explicitly rejects the subject of the Enlightenment understood as an *a priori* subject of knowledge: "What I refused was precisely that you first of all set up a theory of the subject. [...] What I wanted to know was how the subject constituted himself in such and such determinate form."[9]

The subject is an effect, the product of specific power and knowledge constellation. That subject is not prior the history, and not pre-given. It is created and changed by outside events; it

9   Foucault quoted in Margaret McLaren, "Foucault and the Subject of Feminism," *Social Theory and Practice* 23 (1997): 109–27, at 112.

is constantly dissolved and recreated in different configurations along with other forms of knowledge and social practices.[10] This conception of the subject of knowledge as an effect of power and knowledge networks, or this dismissal of the traditional subject of knowledge as one of the central epistemological categories is probably the most radical of Foucault's epistemological moves in his genealogical works. To put it simply, epistemology is not based on the concept of the knower, and knowledge does not have a cause in independently existing knower opposite to the world and other knowers. Foucault rejects the constituting knowing subject of the Enlightenment epistemology. However, Foucault does not reject or abandon the subject completely but he does reject the "philosophy of the subject," the One, universal, disembodied subject, out of space and time, and outside power relations. Foucault's conception of the subject of knowledge displaces the traditional dichotomy between the constituting Cartesian subject, who possesses agency and autonomy, and constituted subject that is entirely determined by social forces. For Foucault, the subject is constituted but it is at the same time the locus of agonism, a permanent provocation to power/knowledge constellation that defines its subjectivity.[11]

By following the similar line of thought, with the idea of the subject created and changed by outside forces and events, in his essay "The Thought of the Outside [*La pensée du dehors*],"[12] Foucault advocates for the way of thinking which accounts for the experience of the "outside"; the way of thinking, which is, according to Foucault, possible

---

10 See also Clare O'Farrell, *Michel Foucault* (London: Sage Publications, 2005).

11 See Katarina Loncarevic, "Foucault's Genealogy as Epistemology," *Belgrade Philosophical Annual* 24 (2013): 65–81, at 75.

12 The article written in homage to Blanchot, "La pensée du dehors," was originally published in *Critique* in June 1966. In most of Foucault's essays that are usually recognized as the ones that belongs to his early works and called his literally phase, he is concerned with transgression of the boundaries of language. They almost all share similar concerns: the notions of exteriority, self—reflexivity and the relation of language to madness and death.

[p]erhaps through a form of thought whose still vague possibility was sketched by Western culture in its margins. A thought that stands outside subjectivity, setting its limits as though from without, articulating its end, making its dispersion shine forth, taking in only its invincible absence […] a thought that, in relation to the interiority of our philosophical reflection and the positivity of our knowledge, constitutes what in a phrase we might call "the thought of the outside."[13]

In this essay, but also in the sentence "I don't say the things I say because they are what I think, I say them as a way to make sure they no longer are what I think," Foucault shows how the utterance of the phrase "I speak" or "I say" problematizes the idea of the supposed interiority of an "I think": "the speaking subject is also the subject about which it speaks."[14]

For him, the work and responsibility of thinking involves an effort to reflect "outside" the already established, limited and codified, historically constituted structures of thinking. This new way of thinking which accounts for the experience of the "outside" — or the "thought of the outside" as opposed to thinking in relation to the interiority of our philosophical reflection and the positivity of our knowledge which always already repeats what is already known — is a kind of *unthinkable thinking* or the *thinking of the unthinkable*. The term *unthinkable* usually refers to the incapability of being conceived or considered, to something that escapes symbolization and representation, to something that is not comparable or that cannot be believed. It can also mean the incredible, inconceivable, or unimaginable — extremely improbable in a way that goes against common sense. The unthinkable is what is beyond the common sense, rationality and generally accepted norms of thinking and doing. The unthinkable thus equals to non-normative, non-legal, or

13 Michel Foucault, "The Thought of the Outside," in *Foucault/Blanchot*, trans. Jeffrey Mehlman and Brian Massumi (New York: Zone Books, 2006), 7–58, at 15–16.
14 Ibid., 10.

even to non-constitutional. The unthinkable is something that cannot find its own name and its own meaning.

In other words, it might also mean that thinking as such makes and reproduces the normativity — that thinking *is* normativity. Does it mean that we *can* think only about the things that we already know? How do we think of change? How do we conceive the political? How do we think the unthinkable?

Coming back to Foucault:

Thinking about the being of language, he claims, opens the subject in the direction of a radical "outside," which destabilizes it and brings it into question. Understood in this manner — according to his interpretation and against the Cartesian tradition of understanding the subject as self-sufficient, self-identical *cogito,* which as such is capable of granting the Truth — the subject is revealed as nothing more than the process of its own disappearance and cancellation. In that sense, the utterance "I don't say the things I say because they are what I think, I say them as a way to make sure they no longer are what I think," indicates that the subject is no longer the sovereign carrier of meaning and significance, but represents a place of opening, exposure and void.

Or, as Jean-Luc Nancy explains, the opening can be understood two ways: "as a wound or as an access route — of entry and exit," and goes on to engage the French notion of "being beside oneself [*être hors de soi*]" in unrecoverability from being exposed to "everything that removes 'us' from 'ourselves,'" that "opens, quite simply, an outside-of according to which we don't come back to ourselves, we don't recover ourselves, nor do we find ourselves." Nancy further concludes that this place of opening, exposure and void is a detour "to that of the other which is outside or is done outside, that is, not the presence of another before me (with its own 'inside') but non-closure, non-return to the self, neither of the other, nor of me."[15]

15 See the interview with Jean-Luc Nancy, "The Real Outside Is 'At the Heart' of the Inside," *Atopia,* 2007, http://www.rave.ca/en/journals_info/1432/moohk/.

The being of language can appear only if the subject is dead in all of its forms. According to Foucault, this, however, as it was already mentioned before, requires a novel model of thinking, perhaps through a form of thinking which is "outside" of subjectivity and which articulates and announces its own end; a thinking that recognizes its own disappearance as inevitable and its contours as *the thought of the outside*. This thinking is about the absolute, radical outside as opposed to the "inside" of the traditional understanding of the subject, but at the same time also as the radical outside of every possible "inside."

This radical outside contains no inner essence whatsoever, and neither does it have presence in any positive sense which would allow a sovereign subject to master over it or to posses it within its own subjectivity. Also, the subject cannot appropriate the outside; the very idea of the appropriation of what is outside of the subject, according to Foucault, would imply one of the two disputable understandings of the notion of the inside: first one of them implies some sort of the inner nature of the outside which could be appropriated, and the second one implies the idea of the inside of this "I" which could gain its integrity precisely through appropriation of the outside. "I" forever remains, argues Foucault, that irreversibly outside of the outer.

> The inside as the operation of the outside: in all his work Foucault seems haunted by this theme of an inside which is merely the fold of the outside, as if a ship were a folding of the sea.[16]

Thinking of/as the experience of the outside is thus the experience of/as (one's own) undoing, which exposes the subject to everything that might threaten or question it; that might change it.

Thinking understood in such a manner, Foucault argues, could be considered as dangerous act since the outside can only be experienced in the process of one's own doubling, undoing, becoming the other.

16 Deleuze, *Foucault,* 81.

But the double is never a projection of the interior; on the contrary, it is an interiorization of the outside. It is not a doubling of the One, but a redoubling of the Other. It is not a reproduction of the Same, but a repetition of the Different. It is not the emanation of an I, but something that places in immanence an always other or a Non-self. It is never the other who is a double in the doubling process, it is a self that lives me as the double of the other: I do not encounter myself on the outside, I find the other in me ("it is always concerned with showing how the Other, the Distant, is also the Near and the Same").[17]

17 Ibid., 98.

Who is the Other Woman in the Context of Transfeminist, Transmigrant, and Transgender Struggles in Global Capitalism?

Marina Gržinić

I will attempt to answer the question of who the other woman is in the context of transfeminist, transmigrant, and transgender struggles in global capitalism while addressing the status of new realism in philosophy in the same context.

Introduction

I want to elaborate on the above questions in the light of the discussion on decolonial feminist thought while addressing some of the geopolitical spaces outside of Europe, or, more precisely, spaces outside the European Union (EU). I want to argue that this provincial, racist, colonial, and anti-Semitic space of the European Union that consists of a long list of "former" West states as Germany, Austria, Spain, Great Britain, etc. (the list of all the "former West" states, as they like to call themselves, is too long), is in urgent need of a radical transmigrant, transfeminist, and transgender decolonial approach.

It is therefore necessary to intensify the political vocabulary used in our analysis of what the theoreticians of the decolonial turn (theoreticians formed by Latin American and US/Latin American context at the beginning of the year 2000) propose as their point of departure. They rightly argue that the *colonial matrix of power* gallops on the back of modernity, or even more precisely, that there is no modernity without coloniality.

The colonial matrix of power, a term coined by Anibal Quijano, should be understood, as exposed by Joaquín Barriendos in his article "Coloniality of Seeing: Visuality, Capitalism and Epistemological Racism," as a hierarchical power machinery that works inside capitalism, but under an explicit form that Quijano names "historical-structural heterogeneity"[1]; in other words, coloniality is a series of inconsistencies, referrals, and reformulations of the hierarchical model of power, which interconnect in its dis-continuity, from the fifteenth to the twenty-first century.[2]

This is the position I take when analyzing the European space, arguing that those analogous categories of race, class, gender, sexuality, nation, etc., continue to fundamentally structure our lives, labor, and epistemologies. The most important question here is: in what way?

Sayak Valencia argues that we have to recognize the structural logic and practice of violence necessary for the functioning of capitalism today, and that because of such logic and practice, we could refer to contemporary capitalism as gore capitalism.[3] This consists in a constant production of subalterns that do not exist *per se*. In this respect, we could state that subalternization is a continuous process, meaning that we have to escape from positions of victimization or from the colonial identity that underpins the threatening presence of the abject. Therefore in agreement with Barriendos, let me say that I do not accept as

1 Anibal Quijano, "Coloniality of Power, Eurocentrism and Latin America," *Nepantla: Views from South* 1, no. 3 (2000): 533–80, at 545.
2 Joaquín Barriendos, "Coloniality of Seeing: Visuality, Capitalism and Epistemological Racism," in *Desenganche: Other Visual Elements and Sounds,* ed. La Tronkal (Quito: Tronkal, 2010), 137.
3 Sayak Valencia Triana, *Capitalismo Gore* (Barcelona: Melusina, 2010), 10. Gore describes particularly vivid and realistic acts of violence and brutality in visual media such as literature, film, television, and video games. It may be real, simulated live action, or animated.

true the presence of the "'bad savage' that should be visible only as a form of denial of a proper existence."[4]

Moreover, global capitalism imposed a process on biopolitics that showed — in the last decade, but definitely after 2001 — that it is simply not enough to talk about biopolitics in order to understand the relation between capital and life, but that it is also necessary to introduce the concept of necropolitics. In "Necropolitics," Achille Mbembe describes the spatial demarcations of the state of exception as the geopolitical demarcation of zones and the more recent mobilization of the war machine.[5] Mbembe concludes his essay by arguing that the concept of biopolitics might be better replaced with that of necropolitics. Therefore, instead of talking about biopolitics, we should talk, in Mbembe's words, about necropolitics. On such a basis, it is possible to demand a firm historicization of biopolitics with necropolitics. For both Mbembe and Giorgio Agamben, the German Nazi state is a perfect example of the sovereignty of death, or, necropolitics; Mbembe also identifies the system of slavery as one of the primary spaces for the enforcement of biopolitics. Mbembe has also shown that, within the colonies, biopolitics as a form of governmentality worked as necropolitics.

In the logic of gore capitalism, as argued by Valencia, the goods are no longer single, undifferentiated bodies and human life. Here it is no longer the body, but rather its destruction that has become a commodity, and capitalism is "only possible by counting the number of dead (bodies)."[6] Within this, there is a "necropolitical marketing" that produces a change in the transformations undergone by the concept of labor in the last forty years, that is, in the transition from Fordism to post-Fordism. In fact, when production is directed towards the production of death (necropolitics, necrocapitalism, and necropower), it is difficult to understand the global production system within the

4 Joaquín Barriendos, "Coloniality of Seeing," 145
5 Achille Mbembe, "Necropolitics," *Public Culture* 15, no. 1 (Winter 2003): 11–40.
6 Valencia, *Capitalismo Gore,* 16.

known analytical frameworks. This new relation between labor and production of death, reduces, as maintained by Valencia, countries like Mexico to "factories producing gore goods for consumption while meeting international practices and recreational demands."[7] This shows that in neoliberal necrocapitalism the apparent exercising of freedom can only be understood, according to Valencia, in the form of one power seizing the other. This creates a parallel power to the state that does not fully subscribing to it, as it is the case in Mexico, where the narco-cartels and the State live an almost parallel life.

Valencia notices that in necrocapitalism the two dystopian figures of necropolitics, context and performativity, seem free or "traveling" in hyper and post-humannarratives, while non-subjects are restrained, exploited, and dispossessed by militarized capitalist economic dynamics.[8]

In the 1990s, after the fall of the Berlin Wall, we witnessed a blossoming of identity politics, one of its most prominent forms being that of multiculturalism, which was seen as a purely cultural phenomenon. Looking back at that period from a necropolitical point of view, I would argue that there is a formative feature to it that has been systematically overlooked: the emergence of the idea of multiculturalism entailed a process of racialization, which functioned as a classificatory matrix that sustained a monopoly on violent classifications by deciding who lived and who had to die. In all these processes, the concept of the "new" human — as outcome of capital's humanization is subsumed under the unfinished project of Western modernization — stays mostly untouched. The West does not want to deal with it, and, accordingly, engages in all imaginable post-human modes of instituting discourses of authority, while leaving the

7   Ibid., 61. We know that Mexico is not only a state of death but also a hype tourist destination.
8   Cf. Sayak Valencia Triana, "Transfeminist Theory for the Analysis of Male Violence and the Nonviolent Reconstruction of the Social Fabric in Contemporary Mexico," *univ.humanist* 78 (2014): 65–88, http://www.scielo.org.co/pdf/unih/n78/n78a04.pdf.

present and the historical modes of Western colonial *de*-humanization largely undiscussed.⁹

New Realism

In order to answer the question of the status of new realism in philosophy — which I connect with speculative realism and object-oriented ontology (and, perhaps the "new materialism") as new, powerful and omnipresent trends in philosophy these days I will refer to Sophie Hoyle's "Collapse: Contemporary Artists Works Exploring Global Divisions of Labour." Here, Hoyle rethinks the question of materiality in what is an evermore pervasive dematerialization of the present moment of capitalism.¹⁰ Consequentially, she uncovers that we are witnessing a new boom of discourses on materiality within strands of contemporary philosophy known as speculative realism and object-oriented ontology. Today, these strands are very influential in the way they view the "new" human and agency.

I side with Hoyle's point when she claims that speculative realism is antipolitical in relation to several critical questions. Or, to paraphrase Svenja Bromberg, to whom Hoyle references, speculative realism orientation "towards accepting or even embracing objectification as in itself emancipatory can be nothing more than a bad joke."¹¹ In response to Hito Steyerl's claim to embrace "objectness," Bromberg exposes that Steyerl

problematically sidelines the classed, racialised and gendered oppressions of capitalist reality. Within this, masses of people have

9   Compare with Marina Gržinić's section in Marina Gržinić and Šefik Tatlić, *Necropolitics, Racialization, and Global Capitalism: Historicization of Biopolitics and Forensics of Politics, Art, and Life* (Maryland: Lexington Books, 2014).

10 See Sophie Hoyle, "Collapse: Contemporary Artists' Works Exploring Global Divisions of Labour" (2014), https://www.academia.edu/8210923/ Collapse_Contemporary_Artists_Works_Exploring_Global_Divisions_ of_Labour

11 Svenja Bromberg, "The Anti-Political Aesthetics of Objects and Worlds Beyond," *Mute Magazine* (July 25, 2013), cited in Hoyle, "Collapse."

never been granted any "subject status" in the first place and are, instead, rendered mere objects or even superfluous, because not productive, for capital.[12]

Hoyle argues that, although speculative realism asks for realism within what is seen as an accentuated dematerialization, it is actually possible to see the opposite. She states that the space that is built in such a way is not outside of judgment, but is instead a space of elevated critique and insider knowledge of art and academic circles, which predominantly tend to be Western, white, and male. Giorgio Cesarale also states that, in addition to being institutionalized and branded, current speculative realist theories present themselves as "weird" and as "other" despite being a mainstream subject matter for a lot of contemporary practices and theories.[13]

In Hoyle's view, it is clear that

> Object-Oriented-Ontology and speculative realism have been taken up by artists in an attempt to find a new means of re-orienting back to the physical, and though it has great potential, it currently manifests many contradictions: as a relatively insular academic term that remains in the realm of the cerebral, and being recuperated by contemporary art [these days].[14]

Furthermore, Hoyle in reference to Maria Walsh exposes that

> Artists such as Mark Leckey, Hito Steyerl, Ed Atkins and Andy Holden are keen to dissolve their subjectivity in order to exist in a non-hierarchical network of things. But could this desire "to get unalienated" be seen as an infantile abdication of responsibility and even, paradoxically, a narcissistic impulse? Object-oriented philosophy insists on the life of objects, a life they deem no more or

12 Ibid.
13 Giorgio Cesarale, "The 'Not' of Speculative Realism," *Mute Magazine* (Feb. 19, 2014), cited in Hoyle, "Collapse."
14 Hoyle, "Collapse."

less valuable than our own. Does this new materialism offer more equitable relations between subjects and objects?[15]

Hoyle concludes that

> recent discourses concerning online and digital media and the physical self tend to be user-focused and Western-centric, not looking at global divisions of labour, where if cognitive labour is an export from the West, primary production takes place in areas in the non-West, as well as ignoring technology divides by socioeconomic class within the West itself.[16]

To put it more simply, a possibility for a proposed new rematerialization exists only within a discourse that would take into account the international division of labor and brutal exploitation that is geopolitically and racially distributed. That means that in the international circuits of labour and exploitation, the usage of poisoning technologies and chemicals for the extraction of precious materials are those that are at the center of all our "immaterial" digitalized technologies. Therefore, such processes of racialization, exploitation, and poisoning have to be at the center of any form of new rematerialization.

The Other Woman

Contrary to the problematic and stiff conceptual opposition of the two complementary, simultaneously exclusive categories of men and women, the concept of transfeminism brings possibilities for transformation. Moreover, homosexual and queer positions in correlation with transmigrant positions offer further upturns for a transformative and transgressive discourse. The possibilities for different constructions of gender and sexuality, as elaborated by Tjaša Kancler in their writings based on the

15 Maria Walsh, "I Object," *Art Monthly* 371 (Nov. 2013), cited in Hoyle, "Collapse."
16 Hoyle, "Collapse."

work of Beatriz Preciado, take distance from the hegemonic discourses of the heteronormative regime, in particular the power
regime of whiteness.[17] According to Beatriz Preciado, sex, specifically, persists as the last remnant of nature, even after technology has completed its task of constructing the body. Consequently, Preciado indicates that in the sense of technological
intervention (technologies of gender) this relation unties the
contradiction of essentialism and constructivism. Thus, we can
replace, as she points out, sex and gender with the word "tech-
nogender," because the bodies can no longer be isolated from
the social forces of sexual difference.

It becomes clear, as argued by Kancler, that in the last decade we have witnessed a process of disidentification with the
category of "woman." In other words, the category of "woman"
as the subject of the historical feminist struggle is being ques-
tioned. This also asks for the deconstruction of masculinity and
male gender ("One is not born man but rather becomes one,"
or "Gays are not men"). Kancler uncovers processes that were
triggered by the fact that lesbians, gays, transgender, intersex,
transsexuals, women of color, and Chicanas took the stance that
the formation of identities is not a fixed category but rather a
process of constant becoming. Moreover, Chandra Talpade
Mohanty exposes that terms such as "Third World" and "First
World" are very problematic, since they can be seen as oversim-
plifying methodologies; however, they do refer to a given world
that traces its own condition of formation and develops different strategies of empowerment.[18] This last point is particularly
important for what we develop here.

In her talk "In the Mix: Race, Whiteness and Gender in Popular Culture," Viennese theoretician Rosa Reitsamer exposes
what is crucial for the new theory performativity and racializa-

17 Tjaša Kancler, "Tongue Untied, Tongue with Tongue: Mining the Binary
    Matrix," *Identities* 10, nos. 1–2 (2013): 14–19.
18 Chandra Talpade Mohanty, "Under Western Eyes: Feminist Scholarship
    and Colonial Discourses," *Feminist Review* 30 (1988): 61–88.

tion that has the modality of a hyper-social racism.[19] However, what is central to see (in a paradoxic way), regarding antiracism by and within the regime of whiteness, is the two relevant moments at work: on the one hand, there is a demand for us to conduct an analysis of the power and performance of that regime, but, on the other, we see that white anti-racism is disturbingly changing into a paradoxical instrument of "white self-love."[20] This is today heavily criticized by black and migrant positions; white anti-racism is increasingly acquiring a form of grandiose anti-racism that goes into the direction of self-promotion, which also transforms into what is termed "charitable anti-racism," that is just a different form of unreflected racism.

A new perspective is necessary for the future, as well as a new context in order to rethink the position of the other woman today in relation to new realism. The term transfeminism is, as presented by Triana, attributed to Diana Couvant, who used it during an event at Yale University in 1992.[21] Along the same conceptual lines, Couvant and Emi Koyama launched a website in 2000 called "transfeminism.org," created to promote a proposed anthology of transfeminism, with the aim of introducing the concept into academia and connecting people in order to work on projects and issues related to the concept. Hence, in such a context, transfeminism can be understood as a migrant and relational movement and as the articulation of both thought and social resistance, which remains a firm response to dominant systems of representation and repression in relation to feminist struggles and the fight for equal rights in certain geopolitically diverse spaces.[22]

Triana reports that transfeminism can be drawn into four major lines of agencies, movements, and demands:

19 Rosa Reitsamer, "In the Mix: Race, Whiteness and Gender in Popular Culture," a paper presented at a public lecture held in the framework of The City of Women Festival in Ljubljana on October 13, 2005.
20 Derek Hook, "Retrieving Biko: A Black Consciousness Critique of Whiteness," *African Identities* 9, no. 1 (2011): 19–32.
21 Cf. Triana, "Transfeminist Theory."
22 Ibid.

1. The US feminisms of color from Third Worlds, composed of Chicana feminists, African American, Native American, Asian American and postcolonial positions.
2. Sexual dissent and epistemic geopolitical shifts from the South that effectuate a reading from queer to cuir [kvir], a wrongly accentuated pidgin pronunciation by the minorities, which is consciously employed.
3. The movement which asks for depathologization of trans identities (STP, International Campaign Stop Trans Pathologization) and the pro-fucking motion in favor of de-stigmatization and legalization of sex work.
4. A key element is to become minority, while being included in migration economic insecurity circles.[23]

Consequently, transmigrant, transfeminist, and transgender struggles have to be put at the center of investigation and contestation of the relations of capital, power and labor, expropriated surplus value and created superfluous populations, the intensified militarization and deprivation of capitalism, and, last but not least, the Western, occidental, white matrix of power, which is the matrix of pure colonial violence.

To conclude, departing from the most influential book in academic feminism and queer theory, *Gender Trouble: Feminism and the Subversion of Identity* by Judith Butler, and taking into account the ideas I have tried to develop regarding realism, wo/man, racializations and necrocapitalism on one hand, and transfeminism and transmigration, materialism and agency, on the other, I will propose another *platform of insurgency* for the new decade of the twenty-first century.

The title of this platform will be *Race Trouble: Transfeminism and Dehumanization,* still to be rewritten in order to discuss the place of wo/man, race, and class in the violent dispossession processes within global necrocapitalism, while also rearticulating political agencies for the future.

23 Ibid.

The Crush: The Fiery Allure of the Jolted Puppet

Frenchy Lunning

O you whom I often and silently come where
*   you are, that I may be with you,*
As I walk by your side, or sit near, or
*   remain in the same room with you,*
Little you know the subtle electric fire that
*   for your sake is playing within me.—*

— Walt Whitman, *Calamus X*[1]

As an adolescent, I could mark time by the incessant epistemes of crushes I had experienced as I careened through junior high school, and beyond. Only a very small percentage of these emotional junkets were actualized as relationships, and most were only a subject of extreme embarrassment at the erotic obsession with an entirely inappropriate, or horrifyingly inexplicable, and thankfully, unsuspecting subject. The whole phenomenon of the crush puzzled me as it was always completely out of my control and never fully explained, except for a "wink-wink" moment in the special girls-only classes on menstruation and "love" that were *de rigeur* for young schoolgirls of the 1960s. But using the very particular apparatus of object-oriented ontology and its excellent mechanism of "allure," I feel I can perhaps abolish some

1   Walt Whitman, "Calamus X," in *Walt Whitman: Poetry and Prose,* ed. Justin Kaplan (New York: Library of America, May 1982), 286.

of the mysterious shame of my youth, and explain its periodic persistence. It is these ephemeral, inexplicable phenomena that are such excellent subjects for this speculative realistic mechanism: those things in the existence of subjects that defy all reasonable explanation.

I will use Graham Harman's explanation of *allure*, "a special and intermittent experience in which the intimate bond between a thing's unity and its plurality of notes somehow partially disintegrates,"[2] as the staging ground for this discussion of the crush, and indeed, in setting up a rather special case of allure. The *crush,* which is defined as "a brief but intense infatuation for someone, especially someone unattainable or inappropriate"[3] — to which I will add the conditions of "unrequited," "unaccepted," and hopefully, "unbeknownst by the beloved" — to further set the proscenium for this special performance of allure.

Caught in this tragicomedy, are two actor/objects: the "lover-object" and the "beloved-object" who fatefully come into a proximity in which the lover-object "recognizes," then obsesses over, the beloved-object. The crush may be an immediate and intense moment that dissipates just as quickly by a change of venue; or worse yet, it may come as an entirely unexpected bolt of lightning after knowing the beloved-object over a longer period of time in which the beloved-object was simply part of a quotidian landscape, and an unknown (by the lover-object) buildup of passion simmering to a slow boil, which lasts for a very long time.

This "recognition," is a recognition of the *qualities* that exude from the object, that is, the "visible symptoms," beyond which a second layer of qualities appear, which Harman contends are born from a "strife between an object and its own qualities, which seem to be severed from that object," further, that "if

2   Graham Harman, *Guerrilla Metaphysics: Phenomenology and the Carpentry of Things* (Chicago: Open Court, 2005), 143.

3   "crush," Google Search, https://www.google.com/search?client=safari&rls=en&q=definition+of+a+crush&ie=UTF-8&oe=UTF-8.

objects are what exude from us, qualities are simply defined as whatever *does not* recede, allowing us to bathe in them at every moment."[4] Harman's sensual description of a "bathing" in the severed qualities of the beloved-object, certainly goes a long way in describing the initial experience in the real world of the lover-object's erotic desire that becomes — through this initial visual and sensual proximity — the "production designer" of the crush. Harman also typifies these severed qualities as entities that break off as "dark agents" operating below the surface qualities of normal visual perception; they are the actors who enter the stage from the side, as the condition of allure directs the laying out of the backstage rigging for the complex ballet to follow: "Yet in normal perception, these objects" — for now the severed qualities have themselves become objects — "are bound up so directly with their carnal surfaces that we sense no distinction between the two realms."[5] Alas, the pathetic lover-object is clueless to the hidden caper that allure and its "enchanting effect not found in normal experience"[6] is now putting into action.

It is helpful to conceive of the stage area of allure as filled with layers of notes and qualities that progressively recede from the highly visible footlights at the far front edge of the stage, where these visible surface qualities perform the initial lure to the action of the play behind the footlights. These surface qualities are very particular aspects of the beloved's body — the nice lips, dark hair, and good "buns" — but it can also be an aspect of their personality or good humor. Yet as we move deeper into the playing area of the stage, behind the footlights, a complex drama ensues as those dark severed qualities begin to confront other objects exuding from the beloved-object, such as the notes. The notes, in Harman's view are distinguished as "the traits of a thing"[7] or, as "qualities of the objects themselves, quite irrespective of our contact with them."[8] That is to say, notes are qualities that maybe

4   Harman, *Guerrilla Metaphysics,* 150.
5   Ibid.
6   Ibid.
7   Ibid., 149.
8   Ibid., 153.

visual, but also may be aspects of the beloved's conjunction of these qualities and notes, the mélange of known and unknown aspects of the beloved's unity of objecthood. And at the very back of the stage withdrawn behind layers and layers of qualities and notes, lies the "shadowy master-object concealed in its inner sanctum," the so-called "withdrawn object," who Harman suggests "can never be touched," yet its qualities that precede it "seem tangible."[9] And Harman describes this process as "the chain of sensual categories [that] is not a single pattern stamped into shapeless matter [...] but resembles an endless knotted rope in which each thing is tied into its nearest neighbor, each form successively locked into further forms."[10]

Yet in a rather poetic section of his book, Harman develops this "knotted rope" to be the "style of things," which furthers an understanding in how these qualities are greeted at the moment of recognition in a crush. He begins with placing the erotic tinge of allure at the level of the fleshy body: "Through our physical bodies and their extension in the form of tools, we are folded into the world in almost lascivious fashion. Our physical bodies represent "a communication with the world more ancient than thought."[11] And further, that at that level, there is the substantial attachment to a sense of realness to our perception and reception of the sensual qualities that extend out into the ether, like feelers on an insect, reaching out in a receptive quest for attachment. This undeniable and inescapable sensual attachment to the real, makes "Our bodies [...] the ultimate form of sincerity."[12] Harman quotes Merleau-Ponty extensively in his explanation of this sincere position within the sea of qualities: "To have a body is already to be folded into the things rather than stand at a distance from them [...] Flesh is the intertwining, interlacing, interfacing of I myself with the sensible world: 'the presence of the world is precisely the presence of its flesh to my

9   Ibid., 73.
10 Ibid., 155.
11 Ibid., 48–49.
12 Ibid., 49.

flesh."[13] And this "flesh-object" that presents a unity of specific notes and qualities that for the self, represents "the self," and other objects as well — then become recognizable as exuding a specificity of those qualities that Harman denotes as *style*: "We can say of any object that it is not a bundle of specific qualities, nor a bare unitary substratum, but rather a *style* [...] A style is never visibly present, but enters the world like a concealed emperor and dominates certain regions of our perception."[14] That is to say, that although some of those qualities that extend visually from an object might present a certain set of related elements or aspects; style, as a sensible condition and recognition, made in the cognition of those visual severed qualities, seems to form a unifying linkage of resemblance, or at the very least, a sense of cohesion that becomes in allure, recognized as a "style," or as Harman puts it, "a stylistic unit."[15] Style is not just visual qualities, but also a performative note. In the entirety of the performance of the object-unit as it intersects with the world-object, that unity of style is "a symbolism in the thing [object] which links each sensible quality to the rest [...] the style of a thing animate[s] its multitude of distinct and isolable qualities."[16] It is precisely that perception of the style of the beloved-object that is *mis-recognized* or *mis-interpellated* as a "match" for the "fool" — the pathetic lover-object in our drama, who is tricked into believing that she recognizes a style from her own script of desired erotic types. And unfortunately, the performance of this tragicomedy follows certain reproductive priorities as Harman describes this inevitable process:

> The world is flesh or element, an electrified medium in which all entities, as elusive styles, generate surfaces of qualities that fuse together or signal messages to one another. In other words, the world is not just made of substances, objects, or styles: it is made up of

13 Ibid., 53–54.
14 Ibid., 55.
15 Ibid., 56.
16 Ibid., 57.

such styles and the flesh by means of which they come into contact, and which thereby serves as the only causal medium between them.[17]

Thus this description of the stylistic unit of the beloved-object as made up of a series of stylistic "parts" that are qualities, notes, and objects radically enmeshed in the electrified medium, form the appearance of a cohesive stylistic unit. This sets up these "parts" as "players" in the drama on the stage for the performance of allure.

However, I propose that the crush represents a special case of allure — a "crush-allure" if you will — wherein the cohesion of these stylistic parts is imagined, "costumed," and projected onto the beloved-object by the lover-object. This imaginary costume of the beloved-object's style structurally resembles Metz's notion of a "scopic regime" — in which "general systems of visuality constructed by a cultural/technological/political apparatus mediating the apparently given world of objects in a […] perceptual field."[18] In our case, this regime is mediated by the desiring lover-object, whose own notes construct phantom severed qualities of an erotic ideal which is produced from an excess of desire, and are then as "masked-severed qualities" fused onto the beloved-object's notes in the play of the crush-allure. Harman describes something similar, paradoxically as an element of humor, as a "splitting apart of the typical immediate fusion between a living creature" and its "adaptable contact with their surroundings and fold back into special private destinies."[19] That is to say, the splitting apart of the beloved-object into its notes and severed qualities, which then disassembles and deterritorializes its unity, thus leaving it open for the lover-object's consequent reassemblage and reterritorializing of a phantom unity according to the

17 Ibid., 58.

18 Martin Jay, "Scopic Regime," *The International Encyclopedia of Communication: International Encyclopedia of Communication Online,* ed. Wolfgang Donsbach, 2008, http://www.communicationencyclopedia.com/public/tocnode?id=g9781405131995_yr2013_chunk_g978140513199524_ss20–1.

19 Harman, *Guerrilla Metaphysics,* 151.

lover-object's script of desire and expectations.[20] But under the conditions of a crush-allure, the lover's scopic regime of desire, whose own notes appear like costumers rushing in for a quick change, masks the unsuspecting beloved's notes to suit the ideal character it needs to play. Harman states that at this point, "allure contends with objects and notes in separation rather than through the usual fusion of the two,"[21] and this holds true, for the beloved-object is unaware that their notes are now actors in a drama that only the lover-object beholds, as "allure, with its severing of objects and qualities, is *the paradigm shift of the senses*."[22]

But what is the nature of this desiring regime whose drama is so profoundly experienced by the lover-object, and although the drama of the crush can extend for years, yet — so fickle — it can also be over in a day? It is tempting to position the crush as a fetishizing of the beloved-object, and perhaps, that can happen. But fetish as a practice has specific realms of object worship, that is, *objects as parts* divorced from their unity that operate via constriction, character, or effectuation,[23] and whose adulation centers around that object as a locus of sexual gratification. It rarely engulfs an entire human object, and generally does not disappear with time. Yet the *obsessional* character of the fetish is apparent in a crush. And there is something so specifically *personal* in that obsession, which Harman suggests as an experience of *beauty*:

> A similar cutting of the bond between an agent and its traits occurs in beauty, in which a thing or creature is gifted with qualities of such overwhelming force that we do not pass directly through the sensual material into the unified thing, but seem to see the beautiful entity lying beneath all of its marvelous qualities, commanding them like puppets.[24]

20 Ibid., 151–56.
21 Ibid., 151.
22 Ibid., 152.
23 Frenchy Lunning, *Fetish Style* (London: Bloomsbury, 2013), 79–105.
24 Harman, *Guerrilla Metaphysics,* 142.

In fact, Harman earlier refers to the lover-object who is "enveloped in helpless or unthinking routines" of obsessive behavior as a "jolted puppet," and a "universal stock figure of comedy,"[25] which is an excellent description of the lover-object in the throes of the crush-allure, staring in the face of the constructed and costumed beauty of the unsuspecting beloved-actor-playing-a-part-object.

Also in this description, Harman acknowledges this split and inference as the reterritorialization of the beauty onto the entity lying beneath all of its marvelous qualities above.[26] Timothy Morton describes this mask as an aesthetic dimension: "Intense yet tricksterish, the aesthetic dimension floats in front of objects, like a group of disturbing clowns in an Expressionist painting or a piece of performance art whose boundaries are nowhere to be seen."[27] The reterritorialized qualities of the beloved create through the illusion of style an aesthetic mirage, as a trickster who is a known crosser of boundaries, and overwhelms the perception of the bedazzled and jolted puppet-lover-object, matching its desire and longing to such an extent that it fails to see the seams and dirty shoes of the costumed mask of the severed qualities projected onto the beloved-object. Locked into a scenario or dance of crush-allure, the lover-object seems to be controlled by something beyond itself.

In discussing this phenomenon of the allure, Harman shifts through many words that imply a magical aspect to the effects on the lover-object in a state of the crush-allure: "bewitching," "fascinating," and "sorcery," all indicating the condition of being "under the spell," which is a perfect description of the condition of the lover-object in a performance of crush-allure. And Morton agrees: "To think this way is to begin to work out an *object-oriented* view of causality. If things are intrinsically withdrawn, irreducible to their perception or relations or uses, they can only

25 Ibid., 133.

26 Ibid., 136–38.

27 Timothy Morton, "Introduction: Objects in the Mirror are Closer than They Appear," *Realist Magic: Objects, Ontology, Causality* (Ann Arbor: Open Humanities Press, 2013), 19.

affect each other in a strange region out in front of them, a region of traces and footprints: the aesthetic dimension."[28] That "strange region," outlines the mask itself; positioned in the center of the stage — in the "hot spot" of the stage lights, where its identity as the "traces and footprints" of its aesthetic, marks the blocking of the dance of the crush allure. Harman also notes this phenomenon of notes within a costumed presence that shields its identity with an applied mask: "Sensual objects are always completely present, they simply are not present in naked form, but instead are clothed in notes stolen from the other, contiguous sensual objects."[29] This dance of clothed sensual note-objects twirling in the center of the stage is indeed a masquerade. However as Morton suggests, "Things are there, but they are not there."[30] Indeed. It is the anxious ambiguity of the paradox between of a sense of unity of the notes of the beloved-object, sharing the stage with the projected and severed qualities of the mask, that pivots both the real and the face of desire in the crush, as in a state of crush-allure, the lover-object is obsessed with the intricacies of the beloved-object's self. And through the revelation of desire, this obsessive need to perceive and attract the beloved-object, creates the "fool'-lover-object — a historically present character of comedic drama — who we watch in cruel relief that it is not *we* who are bewitched.

Yet the term that is also linked to bewitchery that seems to be most handy for Harman, is charm. This term and his adoption of it appear in his chapter on "humor," as one of the two "mechanisms" within which he understands allure to operate. "Within the realm of allure," says Harman, "there is a difference between *humor,* which feels superior to its object, and *charm,* which feels enchanted by it."[31] Charm is defined as: "a trait that fascinates, allures, or delights," but also "a practice or expression believed to

28 Ibid.
29 Harman, *Guerrilla Metaphysics,* 200.
30 Morton, *Realist Magic,* 16.
31 Harman, *Guerrilla Metaphysics,* 142.

have magic power."[32] These two notes oscillate not only between a fascinating aesthetic and magic, but also between comedy and tragedy, a concept long ago associated with dramatic performance. The hilarity of the pathetic performance of the jolted-puppet-lover-object within the play of the crush-allure against the tragedy of impossibility and loss signifies the very kernel of humor, and is all part of the dramatic action embedded within the crush-allure's scenario. It is this special prismatic effect and affect of these severed qualities and notes that dance center stage within Morton's "aesthetic dimension" that characterize and place the charming jolted puppet within the realm of humor. As an aspect within the special case of the crush-allure — this becomes a sturdy foundation: as crushes are generally understood to be "charming" (as long as it is not happening to you), and "comedic," in addition to being "pathetic." These are the very roots of "pathos"; toggling these states in rapid repetitive emotional volleys for the lover-object. Harman describes it as "a kind of magnetic force that realigns our nervous systems. There is often an ambivalence between comedy and this sort of charm, without their being the same thing. One moment I laugh […] and the next I am captivated by the sorcery of its being."[33]

Yet for the jolted puppet, who stands center stage within the masquerade, now deep in the thrall of the masked-beloved-object, a further humiliation arises with the classic theatrical trick of the hilarious-because-uncontrollable gigantic codpiece of revealed, naked, erotic desire which is firmly attached to the jolted puppet's costume — for all to see and for the jolted puppet to suffer. This is a very particular note of the crush-allure: that of *embarrassment*. Embarrassment parses the rotating play of tragedy and comedy, juxtaposing a wicked exposure of desire, with the charm and sincerity that is the pathos of the lover-object as fool. Harman explains this as a mode of vicarious causation:

32 Merriam-Webster Dictionary, s.v. "charm," http://www.merriam-webster. com/dictionary/charm.

33 Harman, *Guerrilla Metaphysics,* 137.

Humans do not really want to be recognized as free and dignified agents. Instead [...] [they] would rather be recognized as stock characters [...]. To be recognized solely as a bare consciousness is actually the root of all embarrassment. It is nakedness as such [...]. Humiliation strips a lowly central agent of its socially recognized powers, leaving only the hapless striving ego on stage [...].[34]

However, for the lover-object, there is also another specificity to the crush allure, a set of conditions and notes that create the very profile of the crush, enjoining the tragicomedy and activating the heat of the crush-allure machine: it is "play." Ludicity, "resides primarily in peoples' relations and interactions [...] whether intra-personal [or] inter-personal [...] [play's] varying manifestations gain their ludic character because of the initial pact established between individuals, which invests the behavior of the participants with this character."[35] A concept made famous by the book, *Homo Ludens* (1938), written by Johan Huizinga, "refers not to a set of specific activities, but to a context, a set of principles around which personal and collective experience is meaningfully engaged."[36] This set of contextual notes provides the motivations for the intense engagements between severed and masked qualities in dramatic action for the lover-object alone: the beloved-object — if playing by the rules of crush engagement — is unaware of the drama surrounding his/her/their body-object. In fact these rules are, according to Huizinga's formula, essential for the existence of "play" notes to be activated. Further, according to these rules, play must lie "outside the antithesis of wisdom and folly, and equally outside those of truth and falsehood, good and evil."[37] Play explodes the

34 Ibid., 213.
35 Conceição Lopes, "Ludicity — A Theoretical Term," Department of Communications and Art, University of Aveiro, Aveiro, Portugal, paragraph 6, http://www.tasplay.org/taspfiles/pdfs/lopesludicitypaper.pdf.
36 Francis Hearn, "Toward a Critical Theory of Play," *Telos* 30 (December 1976): 145–60, at 150.
37 Johan Huizinga, *Homo Ludens: Study of the Play Element in Culture* (London: Routledge, 1980), 3–6.

binary conditions of the real world by being "free"; that is, by being outside the cultural operations of the real world — being instead an "aesthetic parallel world" wherein style is constantly reterritorialized and reordered according to desire of the player-objects. As Huizinga suggests play "creates order, is order. Into an imperfect world and into the confusion of life it brings a temporary, limited perfection."[38]

Yet the most profound note sounded — not only for Huizinga and the "play-notes," but most deliciously for the lover-object — despite the agonizing yearnings, the sighs of longing, and the inevitable unrequited ending — is that this performance must remain secret (with the exception of best friends, of course) — if the beloved becomes aware, it is no longer a crush. Huizinga considered this secret aspect of exclusivity to be the key aspect of play:

> The exceptional and special position of play is most tellingly illustrated by the fact that it loves to surround itself with an air of secrecy […], This is for us, not for the "others" […]. Inside the circle of the game the laws and customs of ordinary life no longer count. We are different and do things differently.[39]

The severed qualities of the quotidian experience are in fact in "play," also masked; as *elements* — that is, as Harman would have it, as "the notes of sensual objects" which in the performance of a crush-allure, "coexist side by side rather than fusing together. Numerous elements are present in consciousness simultaneously."[40] So mechanisms of the elements from the real world are next to — or masked with — the elements of "play," and so that the swiveling or vacillating of societally established rules versus the secret flaunting of those rules in "play," create for the player, a sense of *fun*. It is the fun of this performance of

38 Ibid., 10.
39 Ibid. 12
40 Harman, *Guerrilla Metaphysics*, 195.

crush-allure, that is the lived experience of the lover-object, and a key attribute of Huizinga's theory.

But in considering the actual subjective experience of being the lover-object — a severely jolted puppet — within this ludic state of crush-allure, that hegemony of intensely erotic, poignant, and ridiculous emotion — always seems to be directed and controlled by some sort of superior source deep within the lover-object. It is shrouded by darkened mists of notes unknown and incomprehensible to the conscious reckoning, to a source way in the back of the stage, embedded within the very structural aspect of the theater itself. Harman describes this presence by its methodology:

> This invocation of objects is even the typical stratagem of seducers and manipulators. The seducer mumbles something under his breath, refusing to repeat it when she asks him, drawing her ever further into the clutches of his sham secret — or perhaps the secret is real.[41]

Ignoring for the moment Harman's sexist approach, nevertheless I have come to believe this seducer/manipulator can be no other than that great, elusive, untouchable genius: the "withdrawn object." Not that we can ever fully apprehend it, understand it, or even really conceive the content of its objecthood, or the character of its being — nevertheless, this is no other than the "Grand Guignol" — the "Theatre of the Big Puppet" where;

> People came [...] for an experience, not only to see a show. The audience [...] endured the terror of the shows because they wanted to be filled with strong "feelings" of something. Many attended the shows to get a feeling of arousal [...] there were audience members who could not physically handle the brutality of the actions taking place on stage [as] Frequently, the "special effects" would be too

41 Ibid., 152.

realistic and often an audience member would faint and/or vomit during performances.[42]

Right? Is this not what having a crush is like? Harman insists we cannot ever apprehend the "great director," as it is structurally impossible to turn around to face what is always on the other side of consciousness. Like a Derridean "trace," the "withdrawn object" sits in binary opposition to our pathetic jolted-puppet-of-a-self, exerting absolute control over our strings, forcing our notes and qualities to skip in merry eroticism toward the beloved-object *so totally wrong* for us. Our adoration for the beloved-object is illusionary, but truly experienced, yet seemingly out of our control. Crushes are overwhelmingly considered to be a false love. But for the lover-object it is so agonizingly felt; so obsessively real. Morton explains it this way:

> If there are only objects, of time and space and causality […] the emergent properties of objects—if all these things float "in front of" objects in what is called the aesthetic dimension, in a nontemporal, nonlocal space that is not in some beyond but right here, in your face—then nothing is going to tell us categorically what counts as real and what counts as unreal. Without space, without environment, without world, objects and their sensual effects crowd together like leering figures in a masquerade.[43]

Precisely. Yet who can understand the reasoning of the withdrawn puppeteer behind pulling the strings of the fool? It clearly emanates from the "withdrawn object" of the lover-object, yet as an aspect of the lover-object's self, how can it be so cruel? Harman softens the blow by referring to this dictatorship as being "a strange sort of interference"[44] that occurs "between two moments of a thing's being, one that does not occur at all times

---

42 *Wikipedia,* s.v. "Grand Guignol," http://en.wikipedia.org/wiki/Grand_Guignol.

43 Morton, *Realist Magic,* 19.

44 Harman, *Guerrilla Metaphysics,* 143.

as sincerity does, but one that simply either occurs or fails to occur."[45] This enigmatic statement is trying to parse how the power of the subterranean withdrawn object directs the process of allure, creating the "enchanted experience." But how to protect ourselves from this comedy, or how to retain any pride in this ridiculous drama — we will never know.

Yet are there other moments or applications in the subjective experience where this same masquerade of crush-allure might also appear to cloud our judgment and create an erotic frisson within a lover-object? As an "aesthetic dimension," it might very well explain the experience of the viewer/audience/fan in the thrall of the work of art. Harman states: "Art is granted a sort of magic power, allowing us to confront the impossible depths of objects. Or rather, art is only granted the power of *seeming* to be able to do this."[46] Exactly. The "crush" effect of the art-lover-object's attraction toward an art-object acts in an analogous fashion as does for the lover-object toward the beloved-object — both sets of objects set off a condition of crush-allure, wherein the internal aesthetic notes of the art-lover-object's desire projects a squadron of masking qualities as an obscuring veil center stage to wrap the art-object in a mask that reflects and resembles the art-lover-object's own specific notes of desire, to append the art-object — who/which already in some ways resemble certain of those referenced qualities of the art-lover-object's desires.

As Morton points out, there are other realms of object relation and causality wherein this dance of the crush-allure with its masking notes appears between object relations: "Aesthetic events are not limited to interactions between humans or between humans and painted canvases[…]. When you make or study art […]. You are making or studying causality. *The aesthetic dimension is the causal dimension*."[47] In our case, that causal field is the melodramatic stage of the crush-allure. And the masking veil projected by the art-lover-object can be explained

45 Ibid.
46 Ibid., 105.
47 Morton, *Realist Magic,* 19.

this way: "the aesthetic dimension is the causal dimension, which in turn means that it is also the vast nonlocal mesh that floats 'in front of' objects (ontologically, not physically 'in front of')."[48] These objects can be both and either inside or outside the subject-object.

So it would seem to be that in the center stage area, the gap or spatial extension — which is perhaps an easier way to think of this phenomenon as a *chōrismos*, or "irreducible gap"[49] as Morton as framed it — which is the very realm of this aesthetic dimension, and in the case of any condition of allure, also the moment of causality. Harman defines this moment as "a special and intermittent experience in which the intimate bond between a thing's unity and its plurality of notes somehow partially disintegrates" and creates a "strange sort of interference between two moments of a thing's being."[50] And it is in the condition of the crush-allure, and perhaps even all conditions of allure, that the distant hum of the amatory notes invisibly emitted from the dark, withdrawn suzerain directing the action, creates unique, even quixotic interactions that deliver the magical, if not embarrassing, effects of the crush. For the lover-object, it is the effect of a loss of control: reddened cheeks, speeding heart rates, and the inability to focus on anything but the beloved-object, which are signals emanating from the deep directorial authority of the Grand Guignol, the withdrawn object. For the condition of the crush-allure is indeed the "Theater of the Big Puppet," and we as subject-objects in the moment of the crush-allure, are the jolted puppets in the throes of a vicarious — but fun — causation.

48 Ibid.
49 Ibid., 24.
50 Harman, *Guerrilla Metaphysics*, 143.

(W)omen out/of Time: Metis, Medea, Mahakali

Nandita Biswas Mellamphy

In memory of my father who was a great devotee of the Mad Mother.

> *Medea, the woman, knows that she is going to die unless she calls*
> *out to the Other. "For whoever wants me dead, I can be barbaric."*
> *Faced with panic, one must be able to recreate another world without*
> *common measure with the one that is found to be lacking, not just*
> *return a mediocre blow for blow. "Being barbaric." "Being Medea."*
> — Isabelle Stengers, *Souviens-toi que je suis Médée*[1]

> *By subverting, mocking, or rejecting conventional norms and*
> *opening onto the realm of the forbidden (the realm of "forbid-*
> *den things"), "kaligraphy" — the inscription/incarnation of* Kali,
> *goddess of destruction — stretches one's consciousness beyond the*
> *conventional and socially sanctioned, thereby "liberat[ing] [it]*
> *from the inherited, imposed, and probably inhibiting categories*
> *of proper and improper, good and bad, polluted and pure."*
> — Dan Mellamphy, "Kaligraphy"[2]

---

1 Isabelle Stengers, *Souviens-toi que je suis Médée* (Paris: Empêcheurs penser en rond, 1993), 13. All translations from this text are mine.
2 Dan Mellamphy, "Kaligraphy," in *Serial Killing: A Philosophical Anthology,* eds. Edia Connole & Gary J. Shipley (London: Schism Press, 2015), 135.

> *We are no longer a part of the drama of alienation; we live in the ecstasy of communication. And this ecstasy is obscene. The obscene is what does away with every mirror, every look, every image. The obscene puts an end to every representation.*
> — Jean Baudrillard, "The Ecstasy of Communication"[3]

"What if Truth were an Omen?" I ask (with a nod to Nietzsche[4] — through a glass, darkly). What if Truth were a *Namshub,* a Magic Word/Work, the *nomen* of an *omen*? Such a truth advances here — in this essay — masked as women. Metis, Medea, and Mahakali — first, a Pelasgian Titan, the first wife of Zeus and unacknowledged mother of Athena, who was doomed to be swallowed up whole and usurped by the head of Olympus; second, a foreign priestess of the chthonic Hecate, who (as first told in Apollonius of Rhodes' *Argonautika* and later immortalized by Euripides and Seneca) helps the Greek Jason retrieve the mythic golden fleece, and who eventually murders her entire family and escapes back to Colchis; and finally, a fringe Hindu goddess first worshipped by criminals and outcastes, a dark deity clothed in severed heads, who drinks the blood of her victims and resides in the cremation-ground — one who comes to be adopted as an incarnation of great time (*mahākāla*) or death itself in Hindu religion.

All three are women who are *omens* and mothers who are *others*: that is, each is an outsider (foreign, marginal, outcast) with regard to the contexts/constructs of civilization (all three autochthonous in origin, as we shall see, and portending the subversion of propriety), and each brings about the heretical vision of a death and destruction of order and civility, making it impossible to build an alternate politics from and upon

---

3   Jean Baudrillard, "The Ecstasy of Communication," in *The Anti-Aesthetic: Essays on Postmodern Culture,* ed. Hal Foster (Washington, DC: Bay Press, 1983), 150.

4   "Suppose that truth is a woman — and why not?" (Friedrich Nietzsche, "Preface" to *Beyond Good and Evil,* eds. Rolf-Peter Horstmann and Judith Norman, trans. Judith Norman [Cambridge: Cambridge University Press, 2002], 3).

them. Rather than serving as a ground — as archetypes, ideal types and/or avatars — of subjectivity or of alternative agency, these three (w)omen are strictly speaking abysmal stigmata or wounds:

[T]he puncturing *puncta* that cut into the context qua con-job of culture, revealing the *kha* of *khaos* — that gushing gap, oozing orifice, or terribly terrific tear in the fabric of phenomena (phenomenal fabrications) which wounds the world "as we know it." Stable forms find themselves fissured, fractured, fragmented, and (via this "fragmentation," "fracturing," or "fission') formidably fluid, bleeding beyond their beseeming boundaries.[5]

In the following, I suggest that Metis, Medea, and Mahakali are all associated with *matrices,* and all embody the matrix of *holes* — or (w)hole-matrix — that disjunctively conjoins[6] a fabric or network of relations. Metis's cunning intelligence (*mētis*) is said to involve the "interlacing of opposite directions" producing "an *enigma* in the true sense of the word"[7] that constitutes "living bond[s]"/double-binds which "bind" and "secure" but

5   Dan Mellamphy, "Kaligraphy," 135.
6   Cf. Heraclitus's Fragment 10 on "syllapsis" (Heraclitean synthesis): "that which is whole and not whole, drawn-together and drawn-asunder, harmonious and discordant" (http://www.heraclitusfragments.com/B10/index. html).
7   "It is what the Greeks sometimes call *ainigma* and sometimes *griphos*, for an enigma is twisted together like a basket or a wheel. In one of his dialogues Plutarch writes of the Sphinx twisting together her enigmas or riddles (*ainigmata kai griphous plekousan*), devising the questions which Sophocles describes as *poikila*, shimmering, many-coloured, shifting. The composition of some of the best known riddles reveals the tangle of forms and the shimmering of different colours which give them the disturbing mobility of speech which seems constantly vibrating, never for a moment remaining the same as it was. […] The answer which allows [Polyeidos] to escape from the aporia is the infallible grip with which he catches and binds the shifting and mobile words of the riddle" — (Marcel Detienne and Jean-Pierre Vernant, *Cunning Intelligence in Greek Culture and Society,* trans. Janet Lloyd [Chicago: University of Chicago Press, 1978], 303–4); for more on this, see Dan Mellamphy, "Between Beckett & Bec: The Mètic Hexis and Flusserian Flux of Vampyroteuthis Abductionis," in *Marshall McLuhan and Vilém*

themselves elude capture.[8] Medea too is said to be endowed with *mētis,* the cunning technical intelligence that is itself "net-like" and necessitates a knowing how (i.e., "know-how" [9]) to manipulate the matrix of interlaced oppositions. As living magical nets that gain (rather than lose) their power through the paradoxical contiguity of oppositions (and thus through the eluding and exceeding of definition), all three — Metis, Medea and Mahakali — bind and thus mediate, but ultimately remain unbound and unmediated themselves (and thus undomesticated and barbaric from the point of view of civility and the *civitas*), proceeding by way of oblique rather than linear pathways, by deception, illusion, and contagion rather than by way of logic, law, and legitimacy. Each has been anthropomorphized (that is, made to represent woman, gender, sexual politics of varying sorts), but each is incorrectly deemed human[10] and should instead be con-

Flusser's Communication + Aesthetic Theories Revisited, eds. Melenti Pandilovski and Tom Kohut (Winnipeg: Video Pool Media Arts Center, 2015).

8   Detienne and Vernant, *Cunning Intelligence in Greek Culture and Society,* 41–42.

9   "Right from the start the passage giving praise to the *metis* of the Corinthians and their inventions, *sophismata,* seems inseparable from the myth telling of Athena's discovery of an instrument capable of taming a horse and making it submit to its rider. But this same form of intelligence is then further illustrated by Sisyphus and Medea, the two heroes in Corinthian mythology who are most fully endowed with *metis.* With his artfulness, his gift of the gab, his skill in disguising his promises just as he changes the appearance and colour of the herds which he lures away from his neighbours, Sisyphus, the Death-deceiver, emphasises the proportion of malice which enters into the intelligence of cunning. As for Medea, the first of a long line of women who are experts in the use of poisons, love-philtres, spell-binding magic, *pharmaka metioenta,* she is there to illustrate the importance of the part played in the technical intelligence, which is the subject of this twofold account, by another, darker, aspect, an element of magic, several features of which we have already noted in connection with Athena" (ibid., 189).

10 This is lifted from the final endnote of "Ghost in the Shell-Game: On the Mètic Mode of Existence, Inception & Innocence" *The Funambulist,* Dec. 3, 2014, n. 35, http://www.thefunambulist.net/2013/12/04/funambulist-papers-46-ghost-in-the-shell-game-on-the-metic-mode-of-existence-inception-and-innocence-by-nandita-biswas-mellamphy/#35, where I refer to Dan Mellamphy, "The Sorcerer's Magic Milieu," *Ozone: Journal of Object-Oriented Ontology* 1 (2013), in which he quotes the young Gilles Deleuze

sidered inhuman and overhuman: "If Medea had been avenged, like us simple mortals, she would have paid the price for her act of revenge. She has entered into a contract with humanity and the contract has been broken."[11] This is one context in which we can understand Medea's defiant statement that she can be barbaric[12]; "being Medea" means being untamable, unassimilable, un-anthropomorph(ize)able — that is, being inhuman and/or overhuman.

> [F]our-armed, garlanded with skulls and with disheveled hair, she holds a freshly-cut human head and a bloodied scimitar in her left hands while making signs for fearlessness, assurance, and the bestowing of boons with her right hands. Her neck adorned with a garland of severed human heads all dripping blood, a severed head hanging from each of her earlobes, she wears a girdle of severed human hands round her waist [...] and the smile on her lips glistens with blood [...] as her three eyes burn red, glaring like two rising suns."[13]

Mahakali, as such, might be the clearest articulation of a pre-human and overhuman assemblage which is arguably becoming emblematic of an emergent planetary-wide "network-centric condition":[14] she is always multiple, heterogeneous, and terrifyingly in-/over-human.

who himself quotes the translated Giovanni Malfatti di Montereggio (a.k.a. Jean Malfatti de Montereggio a.k.a. Johann Malfatti von Monteregio), *La mathèse, ou: anarchie et hiérarchie de la science,* trans. Christien Ostrowski (Paris: Editions du Griffon d'Or, 1946), xii:"[doesn't such a mathesis,] however, surpass this 'living human nature'? — [for] it defines itself as [a] collective and supreme knowledge, [a] universal synthesis, '[a] living unity incorrectly deemed human.'"

11 Isabelle Stengers, *Souviens-toi que je suis Médée,* 11.

12 Ibid., 13.

13 David R. Kinsley, *The Sword and the Flute — Kali and Krsna: Dark Visions of the Terrible and the Sublime in Hindu Mythology* (Berkeley: University of California Press, 1975), 1.

14 Dan Mellamphy and Nandita Biswas Mellamphy (eds.), *The Digital Dionysus: Nietzsche and the Network-Centric Condition* (Earth: punctum books, 2016).

So, although all three are personifications and principles of ancient, bygone cultures (*effroyablement anciennes,* in fact[15]), I argue that they are particularly relevant because they conjure and evoke an important aspect of the networked future — particularly, the chthonic[16] matrix that is currently manifesting itself, corresponding to what Alexander Galloway calls not a "hermeneutic" or "iridescent"[17] but a "furious" mediation:

> After Hermes and Iris, instead of a return to hermeneutics (the critical narrative) or a return to phenomenology (the iridescent arc), there is a third mode that combines and annihilates the other

15 *Ancien — effroyablement ancien,* in the words of Maurice Blanchot, which Roger Laporte used as the title for his study of the latter (Paris: Editions Fata Morgana, 1987).

16 From Greek *khthonios* ("in, under, or beneath the earth," from *khthōn,* "earth"; pertaining to the Earth; earthy; subterranean), which designates, or pertains to, deities or spirits of the underworld, especially in relation to Greek religion. The Greek word *khthōn* is one of several for "earth"; it typically refers to the interior of the soil rather than to the living surface of the land (as *gaia* or *gē* does) or to the land as territory (*khōra*) does (cf. http://www.etymonline.com/index.php?term=chthonic). The chthonic here is distinguished from the gaian, from the Greek Gaia, mother of the Titans, personification of "earth" as opposed to heaven, "land" as opposed to sea, "land, country, soil" as collateral form of *gē* (or the Dorian *gâ*), meaning "earth," of unknown origin, perhaps pre-Indo-European. The Roman equivalent earth-goddess was Tellus (see *tellurian*), sometimes used in English, poetically or rhetorically, to designate "Earth personified" or "the Earth as a planet" (cf. http://www.etymonline.com/index.php?term=gaia).

17 "Given the convoluted twists and turns of Hermes's travels, the text is best understood as a problem. Likewise, given the aesthetic gravity of immediate presence in Iris's bow, the image is best understood as a poem. Thus, whereas hermeneutics engages with the problem of texts, iridescence engages with the poetry of images be they visual or otherwise. Hermeneutics views media (of whatever kind, be it text, image, sound, etc.) as if they were textual problems needing to be solved. Yet iridescence views these same media as if they were poetic images waiting to be experienced. […] The culminating moment of hermeneutics is always a type of mystical revelation, a lightning strike. Yet the culminating moment of iridescence is an aurora, a blooming, the glow of a sacred presence" (Alexander Galloway, "Love of the Middle," in Alexander Galloway, Eugene Thacker, and McKenzie Wark, *Excommunication: Three Inquiries in Media and Mediation* [Chicago: University of Chicago Press, 2013], 46, 55).

two. For after Hermes and Iris there is another divine form of pure
mediation, the distributed network, which finds incarnation in the
incontinent body of what the Greeks called first the Erinyes and
later the Eumenides, and the Romans called the Furies. So instead
of a problem or a poem, today we must confront a system. A third
divinity must join the group: not a man, not a woman, but a pack
of animals.[18]

The networked condition that is currently manifesting itself is becoming more and more *furious* ("pack animal"-like),
that is, prehistoric, nonhuman/inhuman, heterogeneous, and
multiple,[19] consequently less and less anthropocentric — i.e., hu-
manistically hermeneutic and descriptively dialectical.

It has been commonplace — even politically necessary — for
feminist theorization since the first wave to ground itself in and
reproduce the conditions for what Baudrillard called "the drama
of alienation," that Primal Scene of Sovereign power[20] in which
a primordial heterogeneity is turned into a difference that can

18 Ibid., 56.
19 "[The Furies] move through contagion. They are called a 'bloody ravening
    pack' by Aeschylus, and often described as animals or swarms. The Furies
    are essentially indeterminate in number [...]. If Hermes is a self, and Iris is
    a life, the Furies are an ecosystem, a swarm, a cloud" (ibid., 57–58).
20 As an encapsulation of the Primal Scene of Sovereign power, see for ex-
    ample Christopher Long's account of the legacy of Metis: "From its very
    beginnings, patriarchal dominion has always established its authority and
    won legitimacy by a subversion of the feminine that arises out of an im-
    plicit recognition of feminine power. Swallowing Metis, Zeus secures the
    stable order of his divine rule; sacrificing Iphigenia, Agamemnon asserts
    his authority as sovereign; denying the Erinyes their vengeance, Athena
    founds the human community that bears her name. Each of these stories
    articulates a dimension of the tragic dialectic of patriarchal dominion: a
    feminine power is subverted in a foundational act of decision designed to
    establish and consolidate patriarchal authority; this act of subversion then
    wins legitimacy by repression as it is designated inevitable and identified
    with the natural order of things" (Christopher Long, "The Daughters of Me-
    tis: Patriarchal Dominion and the Politics of the Between," *Graduate Faculty
    Philosophy Journal* 28, no. 2 [2007], 67–86, at 67). Versions and variations
    of this basic dialectical scene can be found in various feminist discourses of
    the 20th century.

be dualized and disciplined, that is, structured dialectically as the antagonistic and agonistic (i.e., alienating and potentially transformative) relations between two forces, or identities, or parties (e.g., order and chaos, master and slave, self and other, male and female, masculine and feminine, patriarchal and ma-triarchal, hetero and homo, light and dark, inside and outside, etc., to name just a few of the dualities that have been in play for centuries). Dialectics — the contestation between opponents or opposing elements, adopted largely from the inheritance of the ancient Greeks — has been the governing metaphor and model for human action and communication in all spheres from war, policy, and ethics, to poetics, aesthetics, and informatics.

Mythically, this governing metaphor is not just as a descrip-tion for relations of exchange in which one element encounters/ relates to another, but more precisely it is an intellectual mecha-nism for conceptualizing knowledge as the product of a funda-mental asymmetric relation of domination and subjugation in which one element, identified as primary, subjugates and incor-porates, as well as metabolizes and eliminates, another element which it encounters as a "strange externality." In the *Theogony*, just as order subjugates chaos and patriarchy usurps matriarchy, so the victory of the Olympians over the Titans (the old chthonic pantheon) is enacted in a Primal Scene of subjugation and in-corporation that thereafter gets repeated: Zeus swallows his first wife, the Oceanid Metis, thereby initiating the entire drama of the Olympian pantheon. Metis's incorporation and domestica-tion by Zeus is the mythic source for the subsequent usurpa-tion of the chthonic gods by the new Olympian order; Athena, Hermes, Apollo are all said have inherited *mētis* through Zeus's incorporation of Metis's powers; and the chthonic Furies are also thereafter subjugated and coopted by the goddess Athe-na — in the name of her father Zeus Pater — and renamed the "Eumenides" or "kindly ones." This is the drama of alienation that is literally meant to put that which is off-stage (*ob-scena*) onto center stage, and in so doing justify the gesture of politi-cal domestication that founds the Sovereign's power over an Other that is initially encountered as unfamiliar, unknown and external, but becomes familiar, known, and internalized. The obscenity of Metis is transformed through her subjugation and assimilation by Zeus: the strange externality that was Metis, now incorporated by Zeus, becomes the catalyst for the birth of Athena, and, as such, the precondition for the emergence of the quintessential Greek invention, the *polis*.

For so long, this basic dialectical model set the scene for the incorporation and domestication of the obscene, that uncanny other the integration of which founds the scenes and circuits of human communication and exchange. The structure of dialectics, like that of the theatrical scene (as well as of the mirror), sets up a dynamic — the very drama of alienation according to Baudrillard — in which the necessary division and distance between two different but related elements (i.e., subject/object) is posited, reversed, and overcome. The city thus encounters a menacing and ungraspable exteriority, one that makes light of and does not submit to the Laws except on its own terms.[21] Has civilization been able to digest the obscenity of Metis, Medea, and Mahakali?

This drama of alienation and the politics of dialectical subjugation, incorporation and transformation no longer adequately reflect the (hyper)realities of our current network-centric condition, which, as Baudrillard had suggested, depends no longer on a communicative and agonistic model of dialectics, difference and reconciliation, but rather on a protean, interfacial, and reticulated model of contiguity which entails the reversibility between identical things:

> The description of this whole intimate universe — projective, imaginary and symbolic — still corresponded to the object's status as mirror of the subject, and that in turn to the imaginary depths of the mirror and "scene": there is a domestic scene, a scene of interiority, a private space-time (correlative, moreover, to a public space).[22] [...] But today the scene and mirror no longer exist; instead, there is a

21 Stengers, *Souviens-toi que je suis Médée*, 16–17.
22 Baudrillard, "The Ecstasy of Communication," 145–67.

screen and network. In place of the reflexive transcendence of mirror and scene, there is a nonreflecting surface, an immanent surface where operations unfold the smooth operational surface of communication. […] No more fantasies of power, speed and appropriation linked to the object itself, but instead a tactic of potentialities linked to usage: mastery, control and command, an optimalization of the play of possibilities offered by the car as vector and vehicle, and no longer as object of psychological sanctuary. […] [I]t's all over with speed […]. Now, however, it is an ecological ideal that installs itself at every level. No more expenditure, consumption, performance, but instead regulation, well-tempered functionality, solidarity among all the elements of the same system, control and global management of an ensemble.[23]

How is it possible to imagine otherness and alterity outside the schema of dialectical difference and resistance, and within the context of the feedback circuit that is structured like a Möbius strip[24] — no longer a scene of events but an ob-scene and heterogeneous medium/mediation in which, instead of agonisms and antagonisms, there are only environmental modulations, tendencies, and thresholds?

Metis, Medea, and Mahakali are best considered in light of ob-scenity, the (furious) (w)hole-matrix that both mediates and subverts logic, law, and civilized channels, including those of the masculine and the patriarchal, but also — of the feminine and the maternal. As figures that presage not just doom but total destruction, these omens are not mediable/mediatable by *logos* or Olympian logic (the principle of Order); all three are portents of dark and occluded, autochthonous, and underground forces;

23 Ibid., 146.

24 "There is no topology more beautiful than the Möbius strip to designate the contiguity of the close and the distant, of interior and exterior, of object and subject, of the computer screen and the mental screen of our brain intertwined with each other in the same spiral. In the same way, information and communication always feed back in a kind of incestuous convolution" (Jean Baudrillard, "The Vanishing Point of Communication," in *Jean Baudrillard: Fatal Theories*, eds. David Clarke et al. [New York: Routledge, 2009], 21).

and all three make use of many temporalities, weaving ways in
and out of various timeframes (*kairos, chronos, aiōn*), eventually subverting and destroying any stable framework, framed
world, or categorical identity through the cunning and magical
manipulation of the very logic and grammar of that order, using
and abusing identity by way of so(u)rcery (autochthonous and
elemental but occulted powers), and (s)witchcraft (the occult
arts/sciences). [25] These (w)omen who are (m)others, inhuman
and invincible, derive their omnipotence from subverting and
flaunting the strictures of consistency and constancy, paternity
and maternity, marriage and motherhood, literally spilling blood
in order to bleed these institutions dry. Their occult powers are
directly linked to metamorphosis and illusion, and accessed
through magical linguistic manipulations.[26] In this sense, each is
not only associated with the magical forces of speech, manipulation of *logos*/logic, riddles and enigmas, but also with the power
of mutation: each is herself the manifestation and concretiza-
tion of (and catalyst for) the enigma, the riddle, the puzzle and
piège.[27] Like the magical forces of language that they summon to
help their allies and subdue their enemies, Metis, Medea, and
Mahakali are traps (called "*strephomena,* as are the puzzles set
by the gods of *metis*") and nets ("which the Greeks call *griphoi*

25 Cf. Mellamphy, "The Sorcerer's Magic Milieu."
26 Metis is said to be "multiple (*pantoie*), manycoloured (*poikile*), shifting
    (*aiole*)" (Detienne and Vernant, *Cunning Intelligence in Greek Culture and
    Society,* 20). "Medea is said to have cast the glamour: spells that 'fetter the
    eyes' — inclusive of 1) magical incantations that bind and unbind 'curse-
    tablets' (*katadesmoi*), 2) knowledge of 'nonstandard forms of speech' such
    as the *voces mysticae,* 3) the ability to decipher 'unrecognizable symbols' or
    charakteres, as well as 4) abilities to move or change physical objects and
    processes, to change and mix-up 'physical order and appearance' — indeed,
    the word *grimoire*, a secret book of witchcraft and spells containing obscure
    language or illegible writing, is derived from grammaire, of which the word
    glamour is also a derivative" (Amy Wygant, *Medea, Magic, and Modernity
    in France* [Hampshire: Ashgate Press, 2007], 16).
27 lure, ruse, snare and/or trap (*piège* is also a pitfall, a portal to an abyss)
    (http://www.en.wiktionary.org/wiki/pi%C3%A8ge).

[…], the name given to some types of fishing-nets"[28]). As omens that are also enigmas, Metis, Medea, and Mahakali act like *namshubs*:[29] spells (destructive codes/code-words/code-works) that contaminate and destroy *logos* itself — not archetypes of communication *per se* but monstrous aberrations that are harbingers of total logical and semantic breakdown. All three enact what they describe: they are catalysts for and mechanisms of total informational apocalypse (what Scott Bakker calls "the semantic apocalypse" and Neal Stephenson in *Snow Crash* the "infocalypse"[30]), wherein language ceases to be hermeneutically "communicative" and instead becomes "oracular," where "language changes into an oracle"[31] in the words of Michel Leiris[32];

28 "Through her name, Clytaemnestra is connected with *metis*. In her description of the net which she will use to trap Agamemnon and bind him in aporia (Aeschylus, *Agamemnon* 1382), moreover, she also activates the association of *metis* with fishing. This illustrates the complexity and adaptability of the notion of *metis* to different contexts" (Evelien Bracke, *Of Metis and Magic: The Conceptual Transformation of Circe and Medea in Ancient Greek Poetry*, PhD dissertation, University of Maynooth, 2009, 64–65).

29 "Namshub is a word from Sumerian," writes Neal Stephenson in his novel *Snow Crash*: "A nam-shub is a speech with magical force. The closest English equivalent would be 'incantation,' but this has a number of incorrect connotations. […] The nam-shub of Enki is both a story and an incantation" — "A self-fulfilling fiction" (Neal Stephenson, *Snow Crash* [New York: Random House, 2003], 211).

30 Scott Bakker, "The Semantic Apocalypse," *Speculative Heresy,* Nov. 26, 2008, http://speculativeheresy.wordpress.com/2008/11/26/the-semantic-apocalypse; Neal Stephenson, "The Infocalypse," in *Snow Crash* (New York: Bantam Books, 1992), 69, 111, 205, 218.

31 This magical omniscience is not Olympian — it is not the insight of Zeus's second wife Themis ("patron to the oracles of the earth"), for example — but that of Metis, "daughter of Okeanos and Tethys," oracle of the waters. "The divining words of Themis express the necessity, the irrevocability of divine decrees which men can do nothing to avoid. When Metis is consulted as an oracle she speaks of the future from the point of view of a trial between men and gods, seeing it as a subtle and dangerous game where nothing is fixed in advance, in which those consulting the gods must know how to time their questions opportunely, accepting or rejecting the oracle and even turning into their own advantage an answer given by the god in favour of their adversary" (Detienne and Vernant, *Cunning Intelligence in Greek Culture and Society,* 127).

32 As quoted in Mellamphy, "Kaligraphy," 136, n. 31.

or again, what Galloway would call "iridescent" or "immanent" (ex)communication), and then finally infuriated, contagious, viral.[33]

The challenge, then, is to conceptualize Metis, Medea, and Mahakali from the perspective of networks — or more precisely, (w)hole-matrices — rather than from that of dialectics (with its agonistic political model corresponding to what Galloway describes within the context of the Hermeneutic and Iridescent models of communication and mediation). In their most ominous sense (literally as "omen" rather than as "type[s]"), let us think of Metis, Medea and Mahakali as 1) deployments within a magical (i.e., contagious and technical) environment and 2) architects of contingency or "tensegrity" to use a term coined by Buckminster Fuller[34] (i.e., networked hole matrices) who/which

33 Galloway, "Love of the Middle," 57.
34 Take, for instance, Fuller's explanation of the dynamical principles of the geodesic dome or what he calls Geodesic Tensegrity, discontinuous-compression, continuous-tension structures which are networked hole matrices in the way I have here tried to explore: "If we make microscopic inspection of a pneumatic balloon, we will find that the balloon skin is full of holes between its molecular chains, with a secondary and far smaller space continuity of 'all holes' or 'continuous space' between the remotely-islanded energetic components of each molecule's respective atomic nuclear constellations. All these humanly invisible balloon 'holes' are too small for molecules of gas to escape through. Because the balloons skin is full of holes, it is really a subvisible spherical netting, rather than a 'flexibly solid film,' within which the gaseous element molecules are crowded into lesser volume than required by their respective energetic, ecological domains, like fish within a seiner's net. The resultants of forces of all these net-frustrated molecular actions is angularly outward of the balloon's geometrical center — each surface molecule of the interior group of pressured gas has a vectorial action and reaction pattern identical to a spherical chord. In such enclosure of pressured gas, random sizes of molecules, each too large for the spherical molecular netting's hold impinge randomly upon the interior webbing of the spherically tensioned net. There are, therefore, more outwardly pressing molecules and more inwardly restraining net components than are necessary to the structurally resultant balloon pattern integrity. However, in the geodesic, tensional integrity, spherical nets the islands of interior compressional chordal struts impinge in discrete order at the exact vertexes of the enclosing finite tensional network. My independent satellite or moon structures are then the most economical, frequency modulated, dynamic balanc-

themselves function as mechanisms that introduce incalculability and novelty into a system. The obscenity (that is Metis,
Medea, and Mahakali) always risks exposing the susceptibility
of human relations to the fury of Contingency which engen-
ders the very thing that the social order struggles to contain
and exclude. The obscenity functions, as such, like a catalyst for
"phase transition, like that between liquid and crystal, a change
of identity."[35]

To illustrate my point, take Metis for example. From a her-
meneutical and dialectical viewpoint (which, to bring back Baudrillard, revolves around the drama of alienation and transformation), the story of Metis is a narrative about patriarchy,
gender inequality, feminine power and experientiality. Metis,
the epitome of cunning wisdom (*mētis*), described in the *Theogony* as "she who knows most of all the gods and humans,"[36]
is represented as the subjugated female/subjugated femininity/
subjugated foreignness and interpreted as being a strange externality that must be incorporated in order to constitute Zeus's
sovereignty. Only by absorbing her magic "down into his belly"[37]
does Zeus succeed in containing her: the masculine absorbs and
domesticates the feminine. Zeus deploys *mētis* to consume Metis: he tricks her into turning herself into a fly and then swallows her, but she is already with child. This child, Athena, who
later comes out of Zeus's head, will attest that she was begotten
by no mother but only a father.[38] Undigested, Metis is poison

es between outward bound resultants of force and inward bound resultants
of force. The exterior tensional net is a finite system successfully binding
the otherwise randomly entropic infinity of outbound, self-disassociative
forces" (R. Buckminster Fuller, "Tensegrity" [1961], http://www.RWGray-
Projects.com/rbfnotes/fpapers/tensegrity/tensego1.html). See also §700 of
his *Synergetics: Explorations in the Geometry of Thinking*, http://www.RWG-
rayprojects.com/synergetics/print/pc.pdf.

35 Stengers, *Souviens-toi que je suis Médée*, 14.
36 Long, "The Daughters of Metis," 68.
37 Ibid., 69.
38 "There is no mother anywhere who gave me birth, and, but for marriage, I
am always for the male with all my heart, and strongly on my father's side.
So, in a case where the wife has killed her husband, lord of the house, her

(ominous, unstable, and wreaking havoc); but once digested, Zeus tries to not only civilize and politicize her magical force, but once domesticated, also gives it royal status as permanent and universal.[39] And so, cosmic order and sovereign power take root only by incorporating/domesticating/transforming Metis/ *mētis*, she/that who/which would destroy all order and all politics: the new Olympian order begins with the progeny of Zeus and Themis. Themis, not Metis, is the fertile ground from which springs the stable, continuous and regulated world of the Olympian gods. The hermeneutic and dialectical are thus revealed to also be hierarchical:

> [Themis's] role is to indicate what is forbidden, what frontiers must not be crossed and the hierarchy that must be respected for each individual to be kept forever within the limits of his own domain and status. Metis, on the other hand, intervenes at moments when the divine world seems to be still in movement or when the balance of the powers which operate within it appears to be momentarily upset. […] The cunning of Metis constitutes a threat to any established order; her intelligence operates in the realm of what is shifting and unexpected in order the better to reverse situations and overturn hierarchies which appear unassailable.[40]

Thus dialectics cannot fully digest Metis because she cannot be fully domesticated by hierarchies (even reversed and transformed ones). Instead of being hierarchical, metic intelligence is distributed and duplicitous (the French word *duplice* connotes

death shall not mean most to me" (Aeschylus, *Eumenides,* ll. 736–40, in *The Classical Greek Reader,* eds. Kenneth John Atchity and Rosemary McKenna [Oxford: Oxford University Press, 1996], 106).

39 "Not content to unite himself to Metis by his first marriage, Zeus made himself metic by swallowing her. It was a wise precaution: once she had conceived Athena, Metis would — if Zeus had not forestalled her — have given birth to a son stronger than his father, who would have dethroned him just as he himself had overthrown his own father. Henceforth, however, there can be no metis possible without Zeus or directed against him" (Detienne and Vernant, *Cunning Intelligence in Greek Culture and Society,* 13–14).

40 Ibid., 107–8.

both duplicity and duplication *qua* multiplicity): in this case, Metis is both poison — the threat to any established order as the quote above suggests — as well as possible cure (*pharmakon*) that leads to the establishment of Olympian hierarchical order. While Metis, the *pharmakon,* can be incorporated by Zeus, she cannot be allowed to contaminate order, and so must be excluded and held at bay.

Indeed, as Sarah Kofman suggested in her study of cunning intelligence, the entire foundation of Western thought from Plato onward has been firmly anchored to this Olympian sovereign principle which is constituted by the exclusion of cunning intelligence (*mētis*), "that which proceeds by way of twists and turns."[41] Kofman also highlights the connection Plato made in *The Symposium* — following the Orphic tradition — between Metis and Eros, whose coupling produced a son, Poros. *Poros* (the root of the English "porous") can be translated as passage or pathway, but it can also be translated as expedient, or a way out (the correlative term *aporia* being translated as "obstacle"). Metis, as cunning intelligence, is thus linked to multiplicity, incalculability, and the subversion of any limit or hierarchy:

> The family tie between Poros and Metis is an undissolvable link between the path, the pathway, the forging forward, resourcefulness, guile, expediency, *techne*, light and limit (*peiras*). [...] To say that *poros* is a pathway across a liquid expanse is to underline that it is never drawn in advance, always erasable, always to be redrawn in a novel way. We are talking about *poros* when it is about opening up a way where there does not exist or cannot exist any way, properly speaking; when it is about crossing over an uncrossable, unknown, hostile, [and] unlimited world, *apeiron*, that is impossible to cross from one end to the other; the marine abyss, *pontos*, it

41 "Plato, in the name of Truth, would relegate this entire conceptual idea to darkness, and condemn its ways of understanding and practical modalities; in particular, he would denounce its oblique, vague and uncertain processes, opposing them to the one, exact and rigorous science, the philosophical episteme, contemplative by nature" (Sarah Kofman, *Comment s'en sortir?* [Paris: Editions Galilée, 1983], 13–14, all translations mine).

is aporia itself, *aporon* because it is *apeiron*: the sea is the unending reign of pure movement, the most mobile space, the most changing, the most polymorphous, where all heretofore paths that have been drawn erase themselves, transforming all navigation into an ever novel, dangerous and uncertain exploration.[42]

Detienne and Vernant also link *mētis* with the ruses of the sea, especially to the cunning tactics of the octopus and fish.[43] *Mētis* is fluid, mobile, ever-masked, and polymorphous; *mētis* can bind elements but also can escape a bond by transforming itself. *Mētis*'s subversive power or sorcery lies in its capacity to bind and beguile — that is, to manipulate and transform appearances in order to confront a reality the "polymorphic powers [of which] render it almost impossible to seize."[44]

Medea is like Metis, multiplicitous and duplicitous, both poison and cure. Medea — sorceress, killer and healer — is also associated with this form of magic and metic knowledge.[45] Medea is an outsider, a foreigner from Asia Minor, and although Greek women were also associated with magic, the most powerful of the mages were said to be non-Greeks[46] living on the fringe

42 Ibid., 16–17.
43 "Shifting speech" or *poikiloi logoi* — the technical weapon of the sophist and the politician — is "many coiled" or *periplokai*: the twisted "logos of the octopus" which ensnares and/or traps its prey, as "strings of words which unfold like the coils of the snake, speeches which enmesh their enemies like the supple arms of the octopus" (Detienne and Vernant, *Cunning Intelligence in Greek Culture and Society,* 39).
44 Ibid., 5.
45 Bracke, *Of Metis and Magic,* 15. "In the earliest Archaic texts, though Circe and Medea were deities to some extent associated with what would be construed as 'magic' in the Classical period (i.e., *thelgein*), they were primarily represented as goddesses and strongly connected with the entire semantic field of *metis* rather than merely with *thelgein*. A combination of factors, however, led to the decrease of their association with *metis* in favour of an increasing connection with magical terminology in post-Hesiodic Archaic and Classical texts" (ibid., 69).
46 "[T]he image of Persians and other Eastern peoples as Others or "barbarians" flourished in, for example, Athenian drama. Stratton argues that "magic discourse […] emerged at this time as part and parcel of the new discourse of barbarism. *Mageia* — the religion of Athens's enemy, Persia — now

of society.[47] Although Hesiod portrays Medea as possessor of *mētis*,[48] it is Ovid who describes Medea as "the *barbara venefica*, 'barbarian witch*,*' insinuating that Medea practices love-magic and has cast a spell on Jason."[49] Medea is said to cast the "glamor,"[50] a spell which deceives the eyes, connoting magical beguilement. Glamor, like *mētis*, is an "absolute weapon"[51] that is the sorceress's device for counterfeiting nature (which from the sixteenth century onwards comes to be associated with cosmetics, face-painting, and techniques of subverting appearances): "appearance is now fashioned along the lines of a power that is truly and correctly, if indefinably called 'magical.'"[52]

also acquired associations with various characteristics and practices that Athenians regarded as un-Greek and barbaric" (ibid., 54, 25).

47 Ibid., 25.

48 Ibid., 115.

49 Ibid., 28. "Medea's name, whose origin lies in the Indo-European root *med-*, is related to words meaning both 'I intend' or 'I plan' or 'I contrive' and 'plans' or 'schemes' — deriving from *metis*, or cunning intelligence, but which also has a homonym referring to male genitalia; indeed Medea's name can be translated as "cunning female" or "contriver," even interpreted as an alternative for *metis*, rendering Medea yet another emanation from this category" (ibid., 73–74).

50 "In German, its first meaning is still '*der Zauber; das Blendwerk*' ('magic; a binding, dazzling, or deceiving'). The word was originally Scottish. Like *grimoire*, it was a corrupt form of 'grammar' or 'grammarye,' meaning learning in general and occult learning in particular. [...] When the notorious late fifteenth century witch-hunting manual the *Malleus maleficarum* came to be translated into English by Montague Summers in 1928, 'glamour' suggested itself as a gloss on the original's 'prestigia,' defined in part I, question IX — 'Whether Witches may work some Prestidigitory Illusions so that the Male Organ appears to be entirely removed and separate from the Body' — 'A glamour is nothing but a certain delusion of the senses, and especially of the eyes. And for this reason it is also called a prestige, from *prestringo*, since the sight of the eyes is so fettered that things seem to be other than they are. [...] The devil can cast a glamour over the senses of man. Wherefore there is no difficulty in his concealing the virile member by some prestige or glamour." (Wygant, *Medea, Magic, and Modernity in France*, 18–19).

51 Detienne and Vernant, *Cunning Intelligence in Greek Culture and Society*, 13.

52 Wygant, *Medea, Magic, and Modernity in France*, 25.

Medea, daughter of the Colchian king Aeëtes (who was himself begot of Sun and Ocean) and niece of Circe, is priestess of
the cult of the Golden Fleece, a magical object upon which the
political power of the entire kingdom rests, when she meets Jason, a Greek who, with help of Medea's sorcerous powers, takes
the golden fleece in order to advance his own claim to the throne
of his birthplace, Iolcus. Although historical accounts of Medea
vary widely from earliest mentions in the mythic *Argonautika*
to the later Baroque period,[53] she is depicted as practicing both
guile and beguilement, *mētis* and magic, involving murder and
rejuvenation.

At each step Medea's cunning magic helps Jason and her get
out of untenable situations.[54] Medea is outsider, deceiver, mur-
derer, jealous and jilted wife, and killer of her own children;
but Medea also possesses Metis's *technē pantoiē* or "art of many
facets,"[55] and due to her metic and pharmacological powers, by
the sixteenth century, her technical powers come to be associ-

53 "[T]here was by no means homogeneity even in the earliest poetic represen-
    tations of Medea: she is given different husbands, characteristics, and func-
    tions, and is placed in different cities depending on the individual authors'
    agenda" (Bracke, *Of Metis and Magic,* 118).

54 For example, when, in order to help Jason successfully steal the Golden
    Fleece, Medea tricks her brother (who is in hot pursuit) by pretending to
    surrender while Jason ambushes and kills him. Then she has the body cut
    up into pieces and scattered one by one in the sea to delay their pursuers
    (for she knows that by ancient law, the body must be collected for proper re-
    ligious burial). When Jason and Medea return to Iolcus to claim the throne
    from the usurper Pelias (Jason's uncle), Medea infiltrates the city by disguis-
    ing herself as an old woman (that is, she ingests a potion that renders her
    aged and unrecognizable). She then proceeds to convince Pelias that she
    can restore his youthful vigor and then actually persuades Pelias's daughters
    that they must dismember their father before he can be rejuvenated. Medea,
    herself, took no part in the murder of the king of Iolcus. Later, when Jason
    and Medea must flee from Iolcus to Corinth, Medea successfully concocts
    pharmaka and schemes to get revenge on those who have slighted her, like
    her hosts, the royal family of Corinth (whom she has poisoned and burned
    alive) and her own children.

55 Detienne and Vernant, *Cunning Intelligence in Greek Culture and Society,* 18.

ated with the health and medical arts, as well as with alchemy.[56] Guile and beguilement, *mētis* and magic — these are the technical sources for Medea's (s)witchcraft and of her "so(u)rcery":[57] the word *technē*, associated with Hephaesthus's bonds, is given the sense of trick or trap and often can be found alongside the word *apatē*, or "deception"; the consequence of *technē* being ruse — "something that is not what it appears to be."[58]

Medea and Metis both use technical tools such as incantations and potions, as well as shifting words and logic (*poikiloi*

---

56   "Taken from Ovid's *Metamorphoses,* Book VII, the 'Rejuvenation of Aeson,' […] was a powerful theme in sixteenth and seventeenth century visual art, and was believed to transcribe the struggle of medicine against age, the etymologies which were believed to be related to the names of Medea and her father in law Aeson" (Wygant, *Medea, Magic, and Modernity in France,* 37). Medea represents a '"new convergence between rational understanding and occult forces' that enabled the project of rebirth" (ibid., 42–43). Medea, operator of the great alchemical work, "is at once the alchemist, effecting Aeson's death and his rebirth, and the figure of the alchemical process. Eighteenth century commentators are explicit about this. Pernety's *Dictionnaire mytho-hermétique* observes that 'la Toison d'or conquise est la poudre de projection, et la medicine universelle, de laquelle Médée fit usage pour rajeunir Eson, pere de Jason son amant [The golden fleece, once conquered, is the transforming substance and the universal medicine that Medea used to rejuvenate Aeson, the father of Jason, her lover].' In the *Aureum vellus, oder Güldenes Vliess,* Medea's rejuvenation of Aeson is cited as a clear example of her alchemy, and at the same time, she is identified with the moon, an element internal to the alchemical work: 'Kurz, man that in Opere Philosophico auch so eine Medeam, welche von den Weisen ihre Luna genennt wird [In sum, there is also in the alchemical work a Medea, which the alchemists call their moon].' Medea's figuration as a chemical had by this time a certain history. René Alleau described an inscription on a marble plaque, dated 1680, in the square Victor-Emmanuel in Rome, left over from the destruction of the villa of the marquis Palombara. It reads 'Pushing open the door of the villa, Jason discovers and conquers the precious fleece of Medea,' the first letters of which in the Latin spell *vitriolum,* vitriol: the secret shining crystalline body that symbolizes the philosopher's crude matter. The inscription is described as well in a manual of practical alchemy by Eugène Canseliet, one of the best-known of the 20th-century French alchemists" (Wygant, *Medea, Magic, and Modernity in France,* 46–47).
57   Terms taken from Mellamphy, "The Sorcerer's Magic Milieu."
58   Janet M. Atwill, *Rhetoric Reclaimed* (Ithaca: Cornell University Press, 2009), 52–53.

logoi), but in so doing, they also make themselves instruments of *mētis* — that is, catalysts and mechanisms for contingency, ambiguity and the heterogeneous operations that bring about incalculable modulations within any feedback system of rules and results. Using so(u)rcery and (s)witchcraft, they make themselves into heretical forces that subvert hierarchies, be they spatial or temporal. Weaving appearances with shimmering words, they are both masters, and servants of time: on the one hand, their magical *mētis* depends on mastering temporal "know-how,"[59] which is also a "knowing when" — that is, the technical mastery to *switch between* and weave *in and out of* different schemas of time (including *chronoi* or sequential progressive temporalities; *kairoi*,[60] or propitious moments; and *aiōnes*,[61] in the sense of whole lifetimes, entire generations, or existent eternities) in order to blaze a path or forge a way out of an untenable situation — and on the other hand, they make themselves servants of

59 "Over more than ten centuries the same, extremely simple model expresses skills, know-how and activities as diverse as weaving, navigation and medicine. From Homer to Oppian practical and cunning intelligence, in all its forms, is a permanent feature of the Greek world. Its domain is a veritable empire and the man of prudence, of *metis,* can assume ten different identities at once. He is embodied in all the principal types of men who go to make up Greek society, ranging from the charioteer to the politician and including the fisherman, the blacksmith, the orator, the weaver, the pilot, the hunter, the sophist, the carpenter and the strategus" (Detienne and Vernant, *Cunning Intelligence in Greek Culture and Society,* 307–8).

60 "According to some Hippocratic treatises every disease can be cured, if you hit upon the right moment (*kairos*) to apply your remedies. Detienne and Vernant describe the significance of kairos in the art of navigation: [...] *Kairos*, associated with Zeus *Ourios* who represents opportunity, stands for the propitious moment with the good pilot must seize, having foreseen from afar the opportunity which will arise for him to exercise his *techne*" (Atwill, *Rhetoric Reclaimed,* 58).

61 From Late Latin *aeon*, from Greek *aiōn*, "age, vital force; a period of existence, a lifetime, a generation; a long space of time," in plural, "eternity," from PIE root **aiw-*, "vital force, life, long life, eternity" (cognates: Sanskrit *ayu*, "life," Avestan *ayu*, "age," Latin *aevum*, "space of time, eternity," Gothic *aiws*, "age, eternity," Old Norse *ævi*, "lifetime," German *ewig*, "everlasting," Old English as "ever, always'). See http://www.etymonline.com/index. php?term=eon.

and conduits for temporal weaving and switching, the mixing of different times and temporalities for the purposes of guile and beguilement.[62]

Perhaps the most obscene of all three (w)hole-matrices is Mahakali — "Great Kali," mistress of death and destruction — herself the mask of "Great Time" (*mahākāla*) and one of the most maligned of all the figures of the Hindu pantheon, the latter in no small part due to her extreme appearance and behavior which goes beyond the normal limits of propriety and civility. Like her consort Shiva, she is the omen of horrifying terror (*ghora*). Feral and uncontrollable, she is untamable, even demonic: "she is dark as a great cloud [...]. Her tongue is poised as if to lick. She has fearful teeth, sunken eyes, and is smiling. She wears a necklace of snakes, the half-moon rests on her forehead, she has matted hair, and in engaged in licking a corpse. [...] She has two hands and has corpses for ear ornaments."[63] Mahakali, while bloodthirsty and destructive, is also considered in this role (and not in her more beneficent and gentler incarnations) as the (chaotic) guardian of the cosmos, her destructive and uncontrollable powers being the very necessary precondition for renewal and regeneration. She is heterogeneous and multiple: she transforms, splits, or multiplies herself and "tears into her enemies with awful glee [...] She is the distillation of the furious, raw, savage power and lust of the frenzied warrior, and as such she is truly a terrible being, feared by her enemies, to be sure, but a threat to the overall stability of the world itself."[64]

Although she eventually transcends her origins and comes to be adopted as an extreme manifestation of the "great goddess" in the Hindu pantheon, Mahakali, like Metis and Medea, is most often depicted as having indigenous, or non-Aryan origins associated with tribes relegated to the margins of Indian society, a tribal goddess worshipped by hunters and thieves said to live

62 "Mètic métissage" (Mellamphy, "The Sorcerer's Magic Milieu").
63 David R. Kinsley, *Hindu Goddesses: Visions of the Divine Feminine in the Hindu Religious Tradition* (Berkeley: University of California Press, 1986), 81.
64 Ibid., 144.

in cremation grounds (scorning all categories of civilization), [65] and having early associations to the demoness Nirrti, personification of death, destruction and sorrow in the Vedic literature.[66] Later, Kali enters the Hindu pantheon as the terrifying incarnation of the great goddess-warrior, Durga, literally coming out of Durga's head as she steps onto the battlefield.[67] The brutality and blood-thirstiness of Kali is surpassed only by her jocular contempt for life, which makes her a truly invincible force. Like the metic *namshub* that bedazzles but also lights the way out, Kali "blazes like a million rising suns" even in the deepest darkness.[68] The namshub of the great Kali (*Mahākālī*) breaks all convention (in Greek, *nomos*) and all limitation (*peiras*), burning them away in the cremation fires, "the cremation-ground [being] the place where the five elements — the *pancha mahābhūta* — are dissolved."[69]

Mahakali both dwells in the obscene place of phenomenal dissolution and is herself a force of this primordial chaos. As

65 "The term Thug — Thuggee — is derived from Hindi word उग, or *thag*, which means 'thief.' Related words are the verb *thugna*, 'to deceive,' from Sanskrit *sthaga*, 'cunning, sly, fraudulent,' from *sthagati*, 'he conceals.' This term for a particular kind of murder and robbery of travellers is popular in South Asia and particularly in India. [...] The Thuggee trace their origin to the [mythical] battle of Kali against Raktabija; however, their foundation-myth departs from Brahminical versions of the Puranas. The Thuggee consider themselves to be children of Kali, created out of her sweat" (Mellamphy, "Kaligraphy," n. 20).

66 Kinsley, *Hindu Goddesses*, 84–85, 87–88.

67 As Kinsley notes, "the first demon heroes sent forth to battle her are Canda and Munda. When they approach Durga with drawn swords and bent bows, she becomes furious, her face becoming dark as ink. Suddenly there springs forth from her brow the terrible goddess Kali, armed with sword and noose. [...] She fills the four quarters with her terrifying roar and leaps eagerly into the fray. She flings demons into her mouth and crushes them in her jaws. [...] Laughing and howling loudly, she approaches Canda and Munda, grasps them by the hair, and in one furious instant decapitates them both with her mighty sword. Returning to Durga with two heads, she laughs jokingly and presents them to the Goddess as a gift" (ibid., 91).

68 David R. Kinsley, *Tantric Visions of the Divine Feminine: The Ten Mahavidyas* (Berkeley: University of California Press, 1997), 23.

69 Ibid., 88.

this primordial cosmic force of dissolution, the omen of great time (*mahākāla*) and harbinger of the end of time (*kālīyuga*, the age of destruction corresponding to the Greek age of iron), Mahakali is also known as Mistress of Time, and called the "Mad Mother"[70] to her disciples, a mother who is freed from all worldly attachment (*especially* to her children). The weaving that is order (the Greek *kosmos*) "comes to an end in Kali's wild, unbound, flowing hair."[71] She is the force "who wears all things down"; "she consumes all things. Her appetite is unquenchable, and she is utterly undiscriminating. All things and all beings must yield to relentless, pitiless grinding down by the Mistress of Time."[72] Like the great alchemical Fire that both destroys and transforms, as well as illuminates the path of the adept, the *namshub* of Mahakali[73] involves a great *pyrotechnē*: "setting fire to — and/or upon — existents, Kali reveals the existence beyond it, in all its paradoxical confliction, conflagration, contradiction, embracing both its aporia and its porosity: its absolute and absolutely aggressive ambiguity."[74]

There is no escape from the web of Great Time (*mahākāla*), a Time which comes before and goes beyond the human, the geological, and even the astrological; a Time which both dissolves and holds together all conceptions of time. No alternate politics, agencies, identities can be forged from this source because it is, rather, the progenitor of all things:

> At the dissolution of things, it is Kala [Time] Who will devour all, and by reason of this He is called Mahakala [an epithet of Shiva],

---

70 From the *Gospel of Ramakrishna*: "Crazy is my Father, crazy my Mother — and I, their son, am crazy too! Shyama [the dark one, meaning Kali] is my Mother's name. My Father strikes His cheeks and makes a hollow sound: *Ba-ba-bom! Ba-ba-bom!* And my Mother, drunk and reeling, falls across my Father's body! Shyama's streaming tresses hang in vast disorder; bees are swarming numberless about Her crimson Lotus feet. Listen, as She dances, how Her Ankles ring!" (Kinsley, *Hindu Goddesses*, 136).
71 Kinsley, *Tantric Visions of the Divine Feminine*, 84.
72 Kinsley, *Hindu Goddesses*, 140.
73 Mellamphy, "Kaligraphy."
74 Ibid.

and since You devourest Mahakala Himself, it is You who are the Supreme Primordial Kalika. Because You devour Kala, You are Kali, the original form of all things, and because You are the Origin of and devour all things You are called the Adya [primordial] Kali. Resuming after Dissolution Your own form, dark and formless, You alone remain as One ineffable and inconceivable. Though having a form, yet are You formless; though Yourself without beginning, multiform by the power of Maya [illusion], You are the Beginning of all, Creatrix, Protectress, and Destructress that You are.[75]

Metis, Medea, and Mahakali are the architects of this paradoxicality and themselves aporetic architectures that ultimately do not respect or uphold any of the arguments that historically make up feminist critique. And though each has been used in countless ways to revalue just that — an alternative feminism, an alternate politics — I have argued that all are (w)hole-matrices and obscenities that cannot be completely incorporated within a hermeneutic and dialectical schema (without somehow missing the "point" — the *punctum* and the (w)hole-matrix — that each veritably *is*). Each is an exception to the norm and rule of the *polis,* but each is also the master and servant of the matrix of contingency, contiguity and paradoxicality; as such, each is especially suited for thinking about and through the paradoxes of the Age of Destruction (the fourth age of *kālīyuga*), which will intensify and culminate in our age of digital networks.

75 Kinsley, *Hindu Goddesses,* 123 (translation slightly modified).

"Girls Welcome!!!":
Speculative Realism, Object-Oriented Ontology, and Queer Theory

Michael O'Rourke[1]

Word of new intellectual developments tends to travel indirectly, like gossip. Soon, more and more people feel the need to know what the real story is: they want manifestos, bibliographies, explanations. When a journal does a special issue or commissions an editorial comment, it is often responding to this need. We have been invited to pin the queer theory tail on the donkey. But here we cannot but stay and make a pause, and stand half amazed at this poor donkey's present condition. Queer Theory has already incited a vast labor of metacommentary, a virtual industry: special issues, sections of journals, omnibus reviews, anthologies, and dictionary entries. Yet the term itself is less than five years old. Why do people feel the need to introduce, anatomize, and theorize something that can barely be said yet to exist.
— Lauren Berlant and Michael Warner,
"What does Queer Theory Teach us about X?"[2]

---

1   This article was originally published in *Speculations* II (2011): 275–312.
2   Lauren Berlant and Michael Warner, "What Does Queer Theory Teach Us about X?," PMLA 110, nos. 1/3 (1995): 343–49, at 343.

> *Ecological criticism and queer theory seem incompatible, but if they met, there would be a fantastic explosion. How shall we accomplish this perverse, Frankensteinian meme splice? I'll propose some methods and frameworks for a field that doesn't quite exist — queer ecology*
> — Timothy Morton, "Queer Ecology"³

Frankensteinian Meme Splice (or how hot are queer theory and speculative realism?)

I begin with two epigraphs, both of which were guest columns written for, commissioned especially by, PMLA. Although they are separated by fifteen years, they both make some strikingly similar points which are relevant for someone attempting to chart the potential connections or intimacies between queer theory and speculative realism (and in this position piece I'm placing quite a strong emphasis on object-oriented ontology which is just one offshoot of speculative realist thinking). The first thing we might emphasize is the need to pin things down, to say what exactly queer theory is and does and to be entirely clear about what speculative realism is and what precisely it is that speculative realists do. Yet, perhaps the power and virtue of both queer theory and speculative realism, what makes them so compatible, is that neither is a delimitable field. Part of the at-

---

3 Timothy Morton, "Queer Ecology," PMLA 125, no. 2 (March 2010): 273–82. If you are persuaded by my argument that SR and OOO theorists have always been interested in queer theories and committed to antiheteronormative projects, then one could look to Morton's earlier piece "Thinking Ecology: The Mesh, the Strange Stranger and the Beautiful Soul" in *Collapse VI* (Falmouth: Urbanomic, 2010), 195–223, where he says that "Desire is inescapable in ecological existence. Yet environmentalism as currently formulated tries to transcend the contingency of desire, claiming that its desires if any are natural. Organicism partakes of environmentalist chastity. 'Nature loving' is supposedly chaste […] and is thus slave to masculine heteronormativity, a performance that erases the trace of performance" (214). It is important to note that both of these articles appeared before Morton's now famous conversion to object-oriented ontology. See "All you need is love" on his *Ecology without Nature* blog: http://ecologywithoutnature.blogspot.com/2010/08/ all-you-need-is-love.html

traction of both is their very undefinability, their provisionality, and, most importantly, their openness.

Let's spend a little time with the guest column written by Berlant and Warner, a very rich essay which sadly isn't often read or cited nowadays. In 1995 queer theory was arguably at its peak (at least in the United States) and people were calling for definitions, even though, as Berlant and Warner point out, it was barely five years old as a term and a field of inquiry. Queer then was, as they say, "hot."[4] Right now speculative realism is "hot" and the sheer pace (largely thanks to the blogosphere) with which it has evolved, developed, and extended its pincers into and across disciplines, is nothing short of astonishing. If the "birth" of queer theory can be dated to 1990 at a conference at the University of California, Santa Cruz where the term was first introduced by Teresa de Lauretis,[5] then we can locate the "origin" of the term speculative realism to a workshop which took place at Goldsmiths, University of London in April 2007.[6] The perception that queer was "hot" for Berlant and Warner arises from "the distortions of the star system, which allows a small number of names to stand in for an evolving culture."[7] This has also happened with speculative realism and its splinter faction object-oriented ontology where, in both cases, four "star" names stand in for a rapidly evolving field. The "four horsemen of the philosophicus"[8] who are associated with the founding of speculative realism (despite their many differences and divergent interests) are Quentin Meillassoux, Graham Harman, Ray Brassi-

4 Berlant and Warner, "Queer Theory," 343.
5 Teresa de Lauretis, "Queer Theory: Lesbian and Gay Sexualities. An Introduction," *differences: A Journal of Feminist Cultural Studies* 3, no. 2 (1991): iii–xviii.
6 The proceedings of that event can be found in *Collapse III* (Falmouth: Urbanomic, 2007), which includes the texts from Ray Brassier, Iain Hamilton Grant, Graham Harman, Quentin Meillassoux, and questions and answers from the audience. Alberto Toscano spoke at the second event (in place of Meillassoux) but is not generally associated with SR.
7 Berlant and Warner, "Queer Theory," 343.
8 "Diversifying Speculative Realisms," *Archive Fire,* http://www.archivefire. net/2010/06/speculative-realisms-and.html.

er, and Iain Hamilton Grant. And the quartet of object-oriented ontologists are Harman, Ian Bogost, Timothy Morton, and Levi Bryant. But, as with early queer theory, "most practitioners of the new queer commentary [speculative commentary] are not faculty members but graduate students."[9] The accelerated pace with which speculative thinking has grown and impacted upon other fields (both inside and outside the academy and institutionalized disciplines) has largely been because of the blogosphere and the work of graduate students such as Ben Woodard (who blogs at *Naught Thought*), Paul Ennis (who blogs at *Another Heidegger Blog*), Taylor Adkins (who blogs at *Speculative Heresy*), Nick Srnicek (who blogs at *The Accursed Share*), and others. Again, as with queer theory, this "association with the star system and with graduate students makes this work the object of envy, resentment and suspicion. As often happens, what makes some people queasy others call sexy."[10] As we shall see, it is largely the association of speculative realism (and object-oriented ontology) with four *male* philosophers which has made those calling for a queering of speculative thought and a diversification of its interests to become queasy. In a recent Facebook thread on the lack of women in speculative realism, one commenter referred to SR and OOO as a "sausage fest." One could argue, in paranoid fashion, somewhat queasily, that speculative realism is unfriendly to those working in gender studies, critical sexuality studies, neovitalist and neomaterialist feminisms, and queer theory. But, in this paper, in a more reparative frame of mind, I want to suggest that speculative realism and triple-O theory (as Timothy Morton has recently dubbed object-oriented ontology) have always already been interested in and attuned to issues pertaining to gender, sexuality, feminism, and queerness. One could go even further and say that the "perverse, Frankensteinian meme splice" Timothy Morton dreams of has already been accomplished (but that doesn't mean that the work is done, far from it).

9   Berlant and Warner, "Queer Theory," 343.
10 Ibid.

Undefining Speculative Realism

Berlant and Warner write that, in their view, "it is not useful to consider queer theory a thing, especially one dignified by capital letters. We wonder whether *queer commentary* might not more accurately describe the things linked by the rubric, most of which are not theory."[11] Even though SR and OOO are almost always dignified by capital letters (I prefer not to capitalize them in this essay), they too "cannot be assimilated to a single discourse, let alone a propositional program"[12] and I share Berlant and Warner's desire "not to define, purify, puncture, sanitize, or otherwise entail the emerging queer [speculative realist] commentary"[13] or to fix a "seal of approval or disapproval"[14] on anyone's claims to queerness or to speculative realism. Furthermore, I agree with them that we ought to "prevent the reduction" of speculative realism or object oriented ontology to a "speciality" or a "metatheory" and that we ought to fight vigorously to "frustrate the already audible assertions that queer theory [speculative realism] has only academic — which is to say, dead — politics."[15] For me, much of speculative thinking's allure is its openness, its promissory nature, and that much of what goes under its name has been "radically anticipatory, trying to bring a [non-correlationist, non-anthropocentric, even queer] world into being."[16] Because of this very provisionality, and an attendant welcomeness to its own revisability, any attempt to "summarize it now will be violently partial."[17] But we might see some value in the violently partial accounts, the meme splicings, the short-lived promiscuous encounters I'll be trying to stage here in this "position" paper.

11   Ibid.
12   Ibid.
13   Ibid., 344.
14   Ibid.
15   Ibid.
16   Ibid.
17   Ibid., 343.

So, what follows is "a kind of anti-encyclopedia entry."[18] If, for Berlant and Warner, "Queer Theory is not the theory of anything in particular, and has no precise bibliographic shape,"[19] then I would like to suggest — with a willful disingenuousness since after all sr does have a working bibliographical shape which one can easily constitute[20] — that speculative realism and its tentacled offshoots is not the theory of anything in particular either. We might, to paraphrase Morton, say that speculative realism is the theory *of everything*.[21] If we turn speculative realism into a capital-T Theory, we risk forgetting the differences between the various figures associated with it and the variegated contexts in which they work. As Berlant and Warner caution, "Queer commentary [and speculative realist commentary] takes on varied shapes, risks, ambitions, and ambivalences in various contexts"[22] and if we try to pin the tail on the donkey by imagining a context (theory) in which queer or speculative realism has "a stable referential content and pragmatic force"[23] then we are in danger of forgetting the "multiple localities"[24] of speculative realist theory and practice. No one corpus of work (Harman's, for example) or no one particular project should be made to stand in for the whole movement, or what Paul Ennis has recently called the "culture" of speculative realism.[25]

18 Ibid., 344.
19 Ibid.
20 The Speculative Realism pathfinder maintained by Eric Phetteplace is a wonderful resource: http://courseweb.lis.illinois.edu/~phettep1/srPathfinder. html. But it itself is permanently under revision, a construction site, as he adds new names, terms, blogs, books.
21 Timothy Morton, "Here Comes Everything: The Promise of Object-Oriented Ontology," *Qui Parle* 19, no. 2 (2011): 163–90. Tellingly, he refers there to "the effervescent philosophical movement known as 'speculative realism' [note the inverted commas]" as "cool" by which we might understand him to mean "hot" in Berlant and Warner's sense.
22 Berlant and Warner, "Queer Theory," 344.
23 Ibid., 344.
24 Ibid., 345
25 See Paul J. Ennis, "The Speculative Terrain": http://ucd-ie.academia. edu/PaulJohnEnnis/Papers/380565/The_Speculative_Terrain [Paul J. Ennis no longer maintains his Academia.edu profile, but the reader may consult his

If speculative commentary were simply reduced to being the province of one particular thinker, then its multiple localities would be worryingly narrowed and its localities would become merely "parochial" like "little ornaments appliquéd over real politics or real intellectual work. They [would] carry the odor of the luxuriant."[26] If the work of Harman, or Bryant, or Meillassoux is made into a metonym for speculative theory or speculative culture itself, and if they are held to be exemplary cases (either for good or for bad) then what we lose is the original impetus behind speculative realism and queer theory in the first place: "the wrenching sense of recontextualization it gave."[27] And we would leave speculative realism open to charges of political uselessness and glacialization, "the infection of general culture by narrow interest."[28]

But let us, at least provisionally, disambiguate, to use a Wikiism that J. Hillis Miller is rather fond of. Speculative realism describes the work of a very disparate group of scholars (Quentin Meillassoux, Ray Brassier, Iain Hamilton Grant, Graham Harman) reanimating some of "the most radical philosophical problematics" through a "fresh reappropriation of the philosophical tradition and through an openness to its outside."[29] The term was coined by Ray Brassier, organizer of the first symposium on speculative realism, the proceedings of which appear in *Collapse III*. However, Speculative realism is generally considered "a useful umbrella term, chosen precisely because it was vague enough to encompass a variety of fundamentally heterogeneous philosophical research programmes" as Brassier admits in a recent interview.[30] These philosophies, while at once radically

book *Continental_Realism* (Winchester: Zero Books, 2011) — Ed.]. Ennis shares my conviction that speculative realism is alive and well and exists but that it is irreducible to one single definition.

26 Berlant and Warner, "Queer Theory," 345.

27 Ibid.

28 Ibid., 349

29 Robin Mackay writes this on the jacket for volume II of *Collapse* which features essays from Brassier, Meillassoux, and Harman.

30 Ray Brassier and Bram Ieven, "Against an Aesthetics of Noise," *Transitzone*, Oct. 5, 2009, http://www.ny-web.be/transitzone/against-aesthetics-noise.html.

different from one another, could be said to find some coherence in their opposition to correlationist philosophies. To quote the Ray Brassier interview again,

> the only thing that unites us is antipathy to what Quentin Meillassoux calls "correlationism" — the doctrine, especially prevalent among "Continental" philosophers, that humans and world cannot be conceived in isolation from one another — a "correlationist" is any philosopher who insists that the human–world correlate is philosophy's sole legitimate concern.

The Wikipedia entry for speculative realism offers some further shared ground:

> While often in disagreement over basic philosophical issues, the speculative realist thinkers have a shared resistance to philosophies of human finitude inspired by the tradition of Immanuel Kant. What unites the four core members of the movement is an attempt to overcome both "correlationism" as well as "philosophies of access." In *After Finitude,* Meillassoux defines correlationism as "the idea according to which we only ever have access to the correlation between thinking and being, and never to either term considered apart from the other." Philosophies of access are any of those philosophies which privilege the human being over other entities. Both ideas represent forms of anthropocentrism. All four of the core thinkers within Speculative Realism work to overturn these forms of philosophy which privilege the human being, favoring distinct forms of realism against the dominant forms of idealism in much of contemporary philosophy.[31]

A "foundational text" for speculative realism, then, is Quentin Meillassoux's *After Finitude,* a text which boldly insists on the

---

31 See http://en.wikipedia.org/wiki/Speculative_realism. Again we should say that the Wikipedia entry is constantly being revised. According to the Speculative Realism pathfinder, Michael Austin (who blogs at *Complete Lies*) frequently updates this page.

"necessity of contingency"[32] and critiques the post-Kantian pri-
macy of, as Robin Mackay puts it, the "relation of consciousness to the world — however that may be construed — over any
supposed objectivity of 'things themselves.'"[33] Meillassoux calls
his own non-correlationist philosophy a speculative materialism. One strong critic of Meillassoux, Ray Brassier, in his *Nihil Unbound: Enlightenment and Extinction,* yokes revisionary
naturalism in Anglo/American analytic philosophy to speculative realism in the continental French tradition.[34] He terms his
own approach as "transcendental realism" or "transcendental
nihilism"[35] (a position he at least partially shares with critical realist Roy Bhaskar) while the British philosopher Iain Hamilton
Grant works with a post-Schellingian materialism to produce
a speculative nature philosophy that some call "neo-vitalism."[36]
Graham Harman, heavily influenced by the Actor–Network
Theory of Bruno Latour, has long been advancing an object-
oriented philosophy, emphasizing "vicarious causation" which
turns toward objects and demands a humanitarian politics attuned to the objects themselves.[37] So, despite their many dif-

32 Quentin Meillassoux, *Afrer Finitude: An Essay on the Necessity of Contin-
    gency,* trans. Ray Brassier (London: Continuum, 2008).
33 Robin Mackay, "Editorial Introduction," *Collapse II* (Falmouth: Urbanomic,
    2007), 4.
34 Ray Brassier, *Nihil Unbound: Enlightenment and Extinction* (Basingstoke:
    Palgrave Macmillan, 2007).
35 See Bram Ieven's "Transcendental Realism, Speculative Materialism and
    Radical Aesthetics," paper presented at Duke University's Speculative Aes-
    thetics working group, which interestingly is presided over by the feminist
    scholars Priscilla Wald and N. Katherine Hayles and the queer theorist Zach
    Blas. See the program and texts here: http://fhi.duke.edu/projects/interdis-
    ciplinary-working-groups/speculative-aesthetics.
36 See especially Iain Hamilton Grant's *Philosophies of Nature after Schelling*
    (London: Continuum, 2006).
37 See Graham Harman, *Tool-Being: Heidegger and the Metaphysics of Objects*
    (Chicago: Open Court, 2002), *Guerrilla Metaphysics: Phenomenology and
    the Carpentry of Things* (Chicago: Open Court, 2005), *Prince of Networks:
    Bruno Latour and Metaphysics* (Melbourne: Re. Press, 2009), *Towards Spec-
    ulative Realism: Essays and Lectures* (Winchester: Zero books, 2010), and
    Circus Philosophicus (Winchester: Zero Books, 2010). For the best way into
    Latourian Actor–Network Theory see Bruno Latour, *Reassembling the So-

ferences these four thinkers have been most closely associated with the development of what has come to be called "speculative realism," a term Brassier thinks is now "singularly unhelpful."[38] And this should remind us that Teresa de Lauretis, who coined the term queer theory in 1990 dismissed it four years later as a "vacuous creature of the publishing industry."[39] Perhaps the most "cool" offshoot of speculative realism has been object-oriented philosophy (the term is Harman's and dates quite some way back to 1999) and its twin object-oriented ontology (the term was coined by Levi Bryant). Again the four main thinkers associated with this splinter group (Harman, Bryant, Morton, and Bogost) are very different: Bryant has a uniquely Lacanian take on the democracy of objects, Morton works on ecology, and Bogost writes about video game theory and what he calls "alien phenomenology." Ben Woodard has wondered about the "regnant" status of OOO/OOP compared to the many other variants of speculative realism. He asks:

> OOO/OOP will no doubt continue to grow and I often wonder why (besides having multiple prolific internet presences) it is the strangest/strongest of the SR factions. I think the best explanation is that the approach and even name of OOP reeks (justifiably) of novelty and this is only supported by the fact that Harman and others take what they need from philosophers and move on. This is not an attack but a high form of praise. For instance, it would be hard to call any user of OOO/OOP Heideggerian, Whiteheadian or even Latourian (though the latter would be the most probable) whereas Grant could easily be labeled Schellingian, Brassier Laruelleian (though

cial: An Introduction to Actor-Network-Theory (Oxford: Oxford University Press, 2005).

38 Brassier and Ieven, "Aesthetics of Noise."

39 Teresa de Lauretis, "Habit Changes," in *Feminism Meets Queer Theory*, eds. Elizabeth Weed and Naomi Schor (Bloomington and Indianapolis: Indiana University Press, 1994), 316.

less and less so over time) and Meillassoux Cartesian, Badiouian or, against his will but accurate I think, Hegelian[40]

For the remainder of this position paper, however, I want to focus on OOO because those associated with it, particularly Bryant, Morton and Bogost, have been at the forefront of the (often virulent) debates about queer theory, object-oriented feminism and speculative realism.[41] I want to turn now to that brouhaha

40 See Ben Woodard, "Speculative 2010," http://naughtthought.wordpress. com/2010/01/08/speculative-2010/. Levi Bryant, who blogs at *Larval Subjects,* disagrees and says: "I have a somewhat different theory. While the strong internet presence of OOO/OOP certainly doesn't hurt, this is an effect rather than a cause. In my view a successful philosophy has to create work for others and for other disciplines outside of the philosophy. This work is not simply of the commentary variety, but of the variety that allows others to engage in genuine research projects according to — I hate the word, but have to use it — a paradigm." See "New Intellectual Trends," http://larvalsubjects.wordpress.com/2010/01/12/new-intellectual-trends/.

41 Another figure associated with OOO (but from a critical Whiteheadian angle) is Steven Shaviro who has written a great deal about both sexuality and queer theory. He is also one of the leading lights in the nascent field of Gaga Studies where unexpected interventions have been made into OOO debates. To take just a couple of examples: Firstly, Judith Jack Halberstam has described Lady Gaga's *Telephone* video with its "phones, headsets, hearing, receivers and objects that become subjects, glasses that smoke, food that bites" as "an episode in Object Oriented Philosophy [...] whether the philosophy in question is drawn from Žižek on speed, Ronell on crack or Meillassoux on ecstasy, this video obviously chains a good few ideas to a few very good bodies and puts thought into motion." See "You Cannot Gaga Gaga," http:// bullybloggers.wordpress.com/2010/03/17/you-cannot-gaga-gaga-by-jack-halberstam/. Secondly, Kristopher Cannon has described the bulge in Gaga's crotch at the AMA awards from the point of view of the cloth itself: "I think that this example is one which could also bridge several discussions — ranging from gender (and feminism) to sex/ed behavior and objects to art and fashion and avant-garde aesthetics. The object we would see here is the ever-so-subtle (penis-shaped) bulge, appearing when she bends — a bulge afforded by the way her belts, strap(-on?)s, and/or stitched seams align — a bulge she gets because of the clothing she wears. Not only might this be a moment (a la OOO) where the clothing becomes hard because of the way Gaga wears it, but it is also a moment where Gaga gets a hard-on because of the fashions she fetishizes." See "Telephoning the Cloth that Wounds," http://mediacommons.futureofthebook.org/imr/2010/08/04/lady-gagas- phallicity#comment-2120.

about queer theory and the putative non-politics of speculative realism which raged across the blogosphere in 2010.

Queering Speculative Realism

> *Everything populating the desolate wastes of the unconscious is lesbian; difference sprawled upon zero, multiplicity strewn across positive vulvic space. Masculinity is nothing but a shoddy bunkhole from death. Socio-historically phallus and castration might be serious enough, but cosmologically they merely distract from zero; staking out a meticulously constructed poverty and organizing its logical displacement. If deconstruction spent less time playing with its willy maybe it could cross the line.*
> — Nick Land, *The Thirst for Annihilation*[42]

During his live-blogging at *Object-Oriented Philosophy* of the "Metaphysics and Things" conference held in Claremont in December 2010, Graham Harman recounts a question and answer session between Isabelle Stengers, Donna Haraway, and the audience.[43] He says approvingly that Haraway "agrees with Latour that nothing should be allowed to explain anything else away. And certain forms of correlationism make precisely this error [Haraway has clearly read Meillassoux]." She says that:

42 Nick Land, *The Thirst for Annihilation: Georges Bataille and Virulent Nihilism* (London: Routledge, 1990).

43 Stengers is the only woman included in the landmark volume *The Speculative Turn: Continental Materialism and Realism* edited by Harman, Bryant, and Nick Srnicek (Melbourne: re.press, 2010). Harman explains the reasons for this here: "The collection also has great national and generational diversity. Unfortunately, it admittedly has horrible gender diversity (Isabelle Stengers is the only woman in the collection). To that my only answer is: we tried to do better. The invitation list and the contributors list do not entirely overlap. Sometimes people are just too busy, which of course is as good a sign for them as it was unlucky for us." See "Very Close to Publication," http://doctorzamalek2.wordpress.com/2010/12/21/very-close-to-publication/.

Speculative realism is a term I'm still learning to use in a sentence, as if in a school assignment. Speculative realism is the new kid on the block that has adopted a label for itself, which may sound mean, but all kinds of interesting things are going on under that label and so she may want to live on that block. Not enough girls in speculative realism which makes her mad, but she's still curious and seduced by it [Note: Girls Welcome!!!].[44]

Harman concludes that "overall Haraway [is] a bit more condescending than necessary about speculative realism (most of us really like her stuff), but she does sound interested." It is true that Haraway sees speculative realism as a new kid on the block but she is far from condescending. In his own live blog notes for her keynote paper at the same conference Harman himself quotes her as referring to "'the openness or dare of what has been called speculative realism.' Wow, SR is really in the lexicon now" shortly before asserting that "we now have technical–biological capabilities to generate new organisms without heteronormativity, in ways that queer theory has never dreamed of."[45] While Haraway is right to say that SR is a new kid on the block she is equally correct that its appearance on the scene is an invitation, or a dare even, to queer theory to go beyond itself. What she is disappointed by is the fact that so few girls seem to have been invited along for the ride.[46] Harman reassures her that

44 Graham Harman, "Question Period: Stengers and Haraway on Speculative Realism," http://doctorzamalek2.wordpress.com/2010/12/03/question-period/.

45 Graham   Harman,   "Donna   Haraway   Responds   to   Stengers," http://doctorzamalek2.wordpress.com/2010/12/03/haraway-response-to-stengers/.

46 Paul Reid-Bowen has blogged about Haraway and object-oriented ontology and is pleasantly surprized by how many "parallels and resources there are between her work and OOP," especially the Latourian aspects of her writing on cyborgs. See "Haraway and Object Oriented Ontology," http://paganmetaphysics.blogspot.com/2010/01/haraway-and-object-oriented-ontology.html. Perhaps the ideal location for staging an encounter between Haraway and SR/OOP would be to revisit her first book (not often read these days) from 1976, *Crystals, Fabrics and Fields: Metaphors at Shape Embryos* (Berkeley: North Atlantic Books, 2004).

girls are indeed welcome (his exclamation gives this paper its title) and we shall see that quite a few girls have (always) already accepted that invitation.

If this all sounds rather cosy in December 2010, then we need to go back to a furious argument which took place between Chris Vitale (who blogs at *Networkologies*), Levi Bryant, Michael (who blogs at *Archive Fire*), and Ian Bogost in June and July of 2010 about the question of "Queering Speculative Realism." While the arguments were often heated and personal in nature they did have the effect of putting gender, sexuality, and queer theory very firmly on the speculative realist agenda (as well as forefronting the very politicality of speculative realism too).

The trouble started out with Vitale's highlighting the absence of gender and queerness in SR/OOO and how this blunts, in his opinion, the political edge of both. He wrote:

> To what extent do we still need, or continually need, to queer philosophy? Let me be clear on what I mean by this. To what extent do we still need, or continually need, to work against the normative tendency of philosophy to be a predominantly white, male, heterosexual, middle-to-upper middle class discipline? Why is or has this been the case? What are the implications, and even philosophical implications, of this?
>
> Let's even look at the Speculative Realist movement, or the bloggers associated with it. Am I the only one who is "gay" or "queer"? Is there anyone who doesn't get white privilege on a regular basis? Even though I'm Sicilian–American, I get white privilege on a continual basis. Are there any women who regularly blog on philosophy, speculative realism (I can only think of Nina Power, and yet she doesn't really deal with issues related to speculative realism that much...)? And let me be clear about this: I don't think it's a sin to be born a man, or to be hetero, or to have whitish skin. But I do think it's important that if you get a certain type of social privilege, you fight against it. And that means, I think, trying to dissect the way this produces epistemological privilege of various sorts. So, I do think that if the speculative realist movement is predominantly white, male, het-

ero, we need to not only ask ourselves why this might be, but how it
impacts our thought, and what we can do about this.[47]

Bryant responds by saying that he finds Vitale's worries "ad-
mirable" but pointedly rejoinders that "Vitale knows next to
nothing about the sexual preferences or backgrounds of the
various figures in the SR movement (assuming it can be called
a movement)."[48] While I sympathize with Vitale's concerns too,
I would side with Bryant here because queer is as much of a
portmanteau term as speculative realism and is a non-gender
specific rubric which is pitched against normativity, what Michael Warner calls regimes of the normal,[49] rather than hetero-
sexuality. Queerness is a positionality, a posture of opposition to
identitarian regimes, rather than a statement about sexuality of
the kind Vitale makes.[50] Bryant goes on to question Vitale's identity politics and claims that "the overwhelming desire to label or
subsume ourselves under a particular identity, can be seen as
a symptom of how contemporary capital functions. The problem is that this symptom, like all symptoms, obfuscates or veils
the social relations that generate the symptom. The point here
is that we shouldn't concern ourselves with questions of identity, but that we should raise questions about how this particular
form of politics might very well function to perpetuate the very
structure that generates these crises in the first place." Queerness, as Bryant quite cogently asserts, is about a disintrication
from heteronormative and hegemonic regimes. If we insist on
beginning queering speculative realism by labeling ourselves as
"gay" or "queer" (or wanting to know about the sexual orienta-

47 Chris Vitale, "Queering Speculative Realism," http://networkologies.
    wordpress.com/2010/06/08/queering-speculative-realism/.
48 Levi Bryant, "Vitale on SR and Politics," http://larvalsubjects.wordpress.
    com/2010/06/29/vitale-on-sr-and-politics/.
49 Michael Warner, "Introduction" to *Fear of a Queer Planet: Queer Politics
    and Social Theory* (Minneapolis: University of Minnesota press, 1993), xxvi.
50 Vitale makes similar claims about privilege and identity in his long post
    "Queer Mediations: Thoughts on Queer Media Theory," although he is not
    addressing SR there. See http://networkologies.wordpress.com/2009/12/07/
    queer-mediations-thoughts-on-queer-media-theory/.

tions of those who practice it) as Vitale does, then we are very much on the wrong track.

Bryant takes particular exception to a response post from Michael at the blog *Archive Fire* to the original Vitale entry. Michael writes:

> I want to briefly address his specific question with regards to "queering speculative realism."
>
> Overall, I believe we will begin to see a lot more diversity creep into the general thrust of Speculative Realism (SR) when it begins to get picked up by artists, radicals and other non-institutional intellectuals. That is to say, the issue of queering and engendering diversity is more a problem with institutionalized intellectuality as such than with SR specifically. Academia in general is still very much a white-boys club. The issues of privilege, access and univocality — and even aesthetic–ideological preference and distinctions — are deep class issues at the heart of Western society and deeply embedded within our institutional education systems. And I don't think we can expect SR to diversify and become overtly political if it remains entangled in the academic/blogging/philosophy assemblage.
>
> In less words, we can't expect SR to treat the symptom without its adherents (for lack of a better word) first, or also attacking the root causes of a much larger dis-ease at the core of their disciplines. SR will simply perpetuate the problems existent within the institutions that SR thinkers and bloggers are entangled with. Again, diversity will come when SR is "contaminated" from outside the academy and taken up by non-philosophical modes of intellectuality.[51]

Bryant is insulted most by the insinuation that speculative realism is an ivory tower discourse practiced by those in powerful academic positions and that its ideas don't travel very far beyond the confines of the academy. He responds (and again I agree with him, if not caring much for his tone) that OOO is an

---

51 "Diversifying Speculative Realisms," *Archive Fire,* http://www.archivefire. net/2010/06/speculative-realisms-and.html.

open discipline, a dare in Haraway's terms, and that he ardently hopes it will create "projects for other people":

> OOO is among the most open philosophical movements that's ever existed. On the one hand, OOO has generated a large inter-disciplinary interest from people both inside and outside the academy. Not only has OOO drawn interest from rhetoricians, anthropologists, media theorists, literary theorists, biologists, and even a handful of physicists, it has also drawn the interest of artists, activists, feminists, and so on. In the forthcoming collection edited by Ian Bogost and I, *Object-Oriented Ontology,* there will be an article by the performance artist and feminist Katherine Behar, as well as contributions from media theorists, literary theorists, technology theorists and others. On the other hand, through the medium of blogs, we have opened the doors to the participation of anyone who comes along, regardless of whether they are in academia or not. On this blog alone there are regular interactions between computer programmers, office workers, poets, environmentalists, novelists, comedians, and a host of others outside the academy. Michael can go fuck himself with his suggestion that somehow we're trapped within the ivory tower walls of the academy, ignoring anyone who is outside the academy or from another discipline. I, at least, interact with such people every day.[52]

Bryant confesses earlier in the same post that he finds Vitale's question as to what OOO has "to say about race, class, and gender?" irritating. But, as Vitale points out in a further response to Bryant, he then himself goes on to produce a brilliant OOO reading of *American History X* which is responsive to questions of race.[53] Strangely, however, Vitale does not pick up on the very last part of Bryant's post where he utilizes Luhmannian systems theory to describe the way Spivak's notion of the subaltern flags

52 Bryant, "Vitale on SR and Politics." [The book referenced above, to be edited by Bryant and Bogost, "Object-Oriented Ontology," was never (or has not yet been) published. — Ed.]

53 Vitale, "SR and Politics: Response to Levi and Ian," http://networkologies. wordpress.com/2010/06/30/sr-and-politics-response-to-levi-and-ian/.

blind spots in any hegemonic system (be that race, class, gender, or sexuality). "Resituated in terms of object-oriented ontology," Bryant says, "the subaltern is a system in the environment of another system that nonetheless belongs to the unmarked space of that system within which it is entangled." What Bryant is here calling the subaltern could just as easily refer to the queer, and is "something like the politics of the part-of-no-part described by Rancière."[54]

Before coming back to Bryant let us take a closer look at Vitale's "Queering Speculative Realism" post. He argues there that "Speculative Realism, for whatever we think of this name, is mostly a movement which works to bring speculation and science into a greater rapprochement. But what are the political implications of what we're doing?"[55] He goes on to state that speculative realism is far too concerned with the ontological (philosophical research) rather than the ontic (the messy stuff of actually existing arrangements in culture and politics), a charge that has often been leveled against Judith Butler we might add, and that:

> Epistemology and ontology, the current focus of speculative realism, aren't enough. We need a politics and an ethics from this movement, yes? Does SR have something to say about race, gender, sexuality, or global capitalism? Something that comes from a particularly SR ap- proach to the world? It's my sense that unless philosophy develops all these sides of itself, it isn't complete. Must philosophy be complete this way? My sense is that it should be. I'm

54 For more on Rancière's politics of the miscount and queer theory see Michael O'Rourke and Sam Chambers, "Jacques Rancière on the Shores of Queer Theory," *borderlands* 8, no. 2 (2009): http://www.borderlands.net.au/vol8no2_2009/chambersorourke_intro.htm.

55 Harman writes, albeit in a different context, that "there's certainly a lot more potential in OOF [Object Oriented Feminism] than there is in the 'All-Things-Shall-Be-Destroyed-By-Science' wing of SR, which drags its juggernaut through cities, forests, museums, and zoos, crushing all entities and leaving in their wake only the powder of mathematical structure." See "Levi on Reid-Bowen on Feminism and OOO," http://doctorzamalek2.wordpress.com/2010/01/22/levi-on-reid-bowen-on-feminism-and-ooo/.

not sure if my own work does this, but I think it is a challenge to myself that I need to make sure I at least work to fulfill.[56]

While he concedes that speculative realist thought comes "in many varieties," Vitale is concerned that (and he doesn't ex-culpate himself here) "we" underplay "the politico-social sides of philosophy in the speculative realist movement as it stands now." Ian Bogost replies in an equally irascible fashion to Vitale and *Archive Fire* by saying that

> the argument generally goes like this: philosophies need to include political and ethical positions to be complete. Privileges (like race, gender, and class) make it easy to ignore certain assumptions, and the whiteness and maleness and heterosexism of philosophy writ large automatically infects speculative realism, for it is a product of institutions propped up on those privileges.

But for Bogost OOO is always already political insofar as his ap-proach, his turn to objects, "is itself part of the path towards a solution, of paying attention to wordly things of all sorts, from ferns to floppy disks to frogs to Fiat 500s." So, for Bogost, "politi-cal and ethical positions in philosophy and theory [...] are thus, I would argue, fucked (to use a term that is truly populist)."[57]

However, Bryant is far more sanguine about the political and ethical (and queer) potentialities of SR in posts written *before* and *after* the Vitale flare-up.

Let's start with the blog post written after the argument (in August 2010) over the masculinism of speculative realism be-fore circling back to the earlier post (which might have obviated the whole debate in the first place).[58] Here Bryant talks about mess as something we abhor in our research practices, a term he takes from the social scientist John Law, who in his book

56 Vitale, "Queering Speculative Realism."
57 Ian Bogost, "I am not a Marxist," http://www.bogost.com/blog/i_am_ not_a_ marxist.shtml.
58 Levi Bryant, "Unit Operations," http://larvalsubjects.wordpress.com/2010/ 08/03/unit-operations/.

After Method: Mess in Social Science Research makes a case for "quieter and more generous methods."
Bryant writes:

> What we abhor, to use John Law's apt term, is a mess. Everywhere we think in terms of relations between form and content, form and matter, where one key term functions as the ultimate form (which for Aristotle was the active principle and associated with masculinity) and where all else is treated as matter awaiting form (which for Aristotle was the passive term and was associated with femininity). In short, our theoretical framework tends to be one massive metaphor for fucking and the sexual relationship. Of course, it's always a fucking where the men are on top in the form of an active form inseminating a passive matter. And again, that active form can be the signifier, signs, economics, the social, form, categories, reason, etc. What's important for masculinist ontology is that form always be straight and one. I'll leave it to the reader to make the appropriate phallic jokes here.[59]

What Bryant is arguing for is a spreading or diversification of approaches to method and similarly Law argues for "symmetry" as opposed to a phallic ontology/methodology and he calls for a wide ranges of metaphors for both imagining and responding to our worlds (he calls these "method assemblages"). The political stakes of this are that these methods call forth worlds, helping us to both imagine and take responsibility for them (this seems to me to be the very political underpinning of the work of all four main OOO theorists). Among Law's metaphors for imagining and taking responsibility for our worlds are "localities, specificities, enactments, multiplicities, fractionalities, goods, resonances, gatherings, forms of crafting, processes of weaving, spirals, vortices, indefinitenesses, condensates, dances, imaginaries, passions, interferences."[60]

59 Ibid.
60 John Law, *After Method: Mess in Social Science Research* (London: Routledge, 2004), 156.

Moving on from his discussion of our abhorrence for mess in favor of a phallic univocity, Bryant says this:

What the masculinist passion for ground abhors, however, is the idea of a multiplicity of heterogeneous actors acting in relation together. It is not economics that determines all else. It is not biology that determines all else. It is not neurology that determines all else. It is not signs and signifiers that determines all else. It is not cows and roads that determine all else. It is not history that determines all else. No, the world is populated by chairs, cows, neurons, signs, signifiers, narratives, discourses, neutrons, chemical reactions, weather patterns, roads, etc., all mutually perturbing one another in a mesh. In other words, we have all sorts of negative and positive feedback relations between these different spheres functioning as resonators for one another.[61]

We might take from this that speculative realism and queer theory are in a dance of relation with each other, are enmeshed and mutually perturb each other. As Bryant goes on to write: "What we have here is a mesh of non-linearities without ground. What we have here are all sorts of agencies and objects feeding back on one another, modifying one another, perturbing one another, translating one another." And this choreography involves castrating a certain Lacanianism:

What I've tried to formulate is an ontology without phallus in the Lacanian sense of the term; or rather an ontology where phallus is recognized properly as the masquerade that it is (here an analysis of projective identification in the portrayal of woman as masquerade is an appropriate critique of psychoanalysis). The point is not that the signifier and fantasy do not play a role, but rather that we must see the role that these things play as a role among other actors in a complex network of feedback relations. An ontology without phal-

61 Bryant, "Unit Operations."

lus is an ontology where there is no fundamental interpretant, no ground of all else, no final explanatory term.[62]

Bryant then shifts from discussing the phallus to a "review" of Ian Bogost's book *Unit Operations* and his alien phenomenology of objects. He explains that

> in *Unit Operations,* Ian [Bogost] contrasts unit and system. As Ian writes, "Unit operations are modes of meaning-making that privilege discrete, disconnected actions over deterministic, progressive systems. […] I contend that unit operations represent a shift away from system operations, although neither strategy is permanently detached from the other" (3). This asemiotic understanding of unit operations hinges on the fact that "the unit can always explode the constraints of system, or that systems are always occasional, local stabilities from which units can escape to create a new surprise."[63]

The last sentence could just as well describe Bryant's own understanding of subalternity and second order systems discussed earlier.

Bryant wants to focus in on the operation part of unit operations and how this leads to messy creativeness and amongstness rather than phallic univocity. He explains that

> In his early work (I suspect we'll find that he's of a different view once *Alien Phenomenology* comes out), Bogost is deeply influenced by Badiou's concept of the count-as-one (which has been a longtime fascination of mine as well). The count-as-one is, in Badiou, an operation that transforms an inconsistent multiplicity into a consistent multiplicity, literally counting it as one, or transforming it into a unit. The count-as-one is an operation, something that takes place, not something that is already there.[64]

62 Ibid.
63 Ibid.
64 Ibid.

Bryant goes on shortly after to say that

> In short, unit operations produce, they generate a new entity, whereas system operations re-produce, they iterate an already existing pattern or object. This, really, is what is to be thought in the mesh of exo-relations among the heterogeneous actors populating the heteroverse of flat ontology: What are those exo-relations that reproduce existing units and relations and what are the operations that produce entirely new entities or agents? And if we are to think this, we must think a complex interplay of a variety of different types of entities, how they contribute to the production of new entities, and must avoid our phallocentric inclinations that would erect only a single ground of being [...] we must think processes of unitizing without abandoning objects.[65]

What we might glean from this is that queer theory's unit operations produce rather than reproduce, that there is not one "single ground" of queer theory, OOO, or SR, not one single interpretation of what they are or what they do. Instead they are caught in a mesh, are always in relation to each other and in a gravitational mobility toward each other, and that this mess or mesh of "exo-relations" produces a new kind of theoretical creativity where the concrete concepts of OOO and SR can be put to work with and amongst queer theories and concepts.

Now, let us return to an earlier post by Bryant from January 2010 where he anticipates many of Vitale's charges against SR and OOO and rehearses some of these later arguments.[66] On this occasion he is responding to a post from Paul Reid-Bowen, who blogs at *Pagan Metaphysics,* who was arguing for a realist ontology and a feminist metaphysics in the work of Christine Battersby, Donna Haraway, and Luce Irigaray.[67] Bryant forthrightly

---

65 Ibid.

66 Levi Bryant, "Feminist Metaphysics as Object-Oriented Ontology — OOO/OOP Round-Up," http://larvalsubjects.wordpress.com/2010/01/22/feminist-metaphysics-as-object-oriented-ontology-oooooop-round-up/.

67 Paul Reid-Bowen, "Foreshadowing Dundee," http://paganmetaphysics.blogspot.com/2010/01/foreshadowing-dundee.html.

states that he is unconvinced by a feminist metaphysics (since for him there is *just* metaphysics) but he does admit that Reid-Bowen is "on to something here." And what Bryant suggests he is on to is precisely what preempts some of Vitale's later criticisms of SR/OOP. It is worth reproducing in full:

> In the world of cultural studies and the humanities, I think there have been a number of privileged sites that have been directed towards bucking the primacy of anti-realist or correlationist thought than other disciplines by virtue of the nature of the objects that constitute their object of investigation. These theorists have not, of course, in most cases baldly stated their work as a debate between realism and anti-realism, but their work has nonetheless inevitably led them to thinking being in such a way that it is not simply a discourse, language, or a correlation with the human.
>
> Paradoxically, these privileged sites have largely been *marginalized* in the world of academia and the humanities; no doubt because of the hegemony of anti-realist thought or the status of correlationism as the establishment position. Among these privileged sites I would include environmental philosophy and thought, science and technology studies, critical animal theory, geographical studies, writing technology studies, media studies, *queer theory,* and, of course, feminist philosophy and thought. I am sure that there are many others that don't immediately come to mind for me. If these have been privileged sites for the development of significant conceptual innovations in the field of realist ontology, then this is because all of these sites of investigation force encounters with real and nonhuman objects and actors that cannot be reduced to correlates of human thought, language, perception, or use but that have to be approached in their own autonomous being to properly be thought.[68]

---

68 Bryant, "Feminist Metaphysics as Object-Oriented Ontology" (my emphasis).

After perhaps somewhat unfairly setting Judith Butler's work to one side because, for him, she places far too much emphasis on discursivity,[69] he argues that

> feminist thought (and here I am not even beginning to do justice to the richness and sophistication of this thought and what has arisen out of those inquiries) forces an encounter with the real of the biological body and the difference it introduces into the world, the real of the sexed body, that exceeds the being of the phenomenological lived body and the discursive body, while somehow still being intertwined with these other two bodies [...] the forgetting of the real is always a masculine gesture.[70]

The most crucial point Bryant makes here, however, is that queer theory, among the other "privileged sites" he mentions above, is, although being a marginalized site of realist thought, "in so many respects, *ground-zero* for object-oriented ontology." This is a remarkable assertion: no ooo without queer theory, no sr without queer theory.

oof: *Object-Oriented Feminism*

One of the newest kids on the ooo block is object-oriented feminism, another of Bryant's privileged if marginalized sites for realist thought where the "'really real' is placed on neither the side of the natural, nor the human." Graham Harman humbly admits that he "wouldn't know how to go about constructing"[71] an object-oriented feminism but Ian Bogost has blogged the proceedings of a conference as well as his response to all six pa-

---

69 There is a fascinating moment in *Undoing Gender* where Butler promises to write in the future about "the place of sharp machines" and "the technology of the knife in debates about intersexuality and transsexuality alike": *Undoing Gender* (London: Routledge, 2004), 64. But she never has, at least to my knowledge, written about this.

70 Bryant, "Feminist Metaphysics as Object-Oriented Ontology."

71 Graham Harman, "Object-Oriented Feminism," http://doctorzamalek2.wordpress.com/2010/10/30/object-oriented-feminism/.

pers on this very topic held in Indianopolis in October 2010. The two panels, organized by Katherine Behar, whom Bryant mentioned in his response to Vitale above, took up the question, "what would a program for object-oriented feminism (OOF) entail?"[72] Drawing on Bill Brown's "Thing Theory,"[73] Wendy Hui Kyong Chun used "softwarification" as a way into reconfiguring the relationship between subjects and objects, linking software's "historical emergence as invisibly visible (or visibly invisible) object" to gendered "hierarchies embedded in its vapory structure." Patricia Ticineto Clough, whose earlier work on Deleuze and affect was already making these object-oriented moves, tried to rethink "the relationship of language and a subject" while also bringing to the fore "questions about bodies, desires, phantasms." In the brilliantly titled "Facing Necrophilia, or 'Botox Ethics,'" Katherine Behar picked up Catherine Malabou's notion of plasticity, the ways in which it is able to receive or create form and is situated between the extreme points of taking and annihilating form, to queer the relationship between living and dead objects:[74]

72 The panels was held at the 2010 Society for Literature and the Arts Conference. The first panel dealt with general responses to the organizer's question and the second panel focused in on the theme of the body. There were two responses from Katherine Hayles and Bogost. You can read all six abstracts and Bogost's response here: Ian Bogost, "Object Oriented Feminism," http://www.bogost.com/blog/object-oriented_feminism_1.shtml.

73 Bill Brown has somewhat apologetically developed "thing theory" in such a way that its necessity becomes visible and we could add it to Bryant's list of privileged if marginalized sites for realist thinking which falls out with the correlationist circle: "Is there something perverse, if not archly insistent, about complicating things with theory? Do we really need anything like thing theory the way we need narrative theory or cultural theory, queer theory or discourse theory? Why not let things alone?" In Bill Brown (ed.), *Things* (Chicago: University of Chicago Press, 2004), 1.

74 Malabou's name is rarely invoked in speculative realist (or indeed in queer theoretical) circles but her idea of plasticity is attractive precisely because it is an agent of disobedience, a refusal to submit to a model. See her *What Should We Do with Our Brain?*, trans. Sebastian Rand (New York: Fordham University Press, 2008).

Just as Object-Oriented Feminism incorporates human and nonhuman objects, it must extend between living objects and dead ones.
This paper explores how self-objectifying practitioners of body art
and plastic surgery incorporate inertness and deadness within the
living self. First we discuss body art and plastic surgery through
Catherine Malabou's concept of brain plasticity, the constitution of
oneself through passive reception and active annihilation of form.
Malabou associates plasticity's destructive aspect with plastic explo-
sives and its malleable aspect with sculpture and plastic surgery. Yet
seen from under the knife, plastic surgery and body art seem to
make plastic objects in Malabou's full sense of the term. The plastic
art object of surgery kills off its old self to sculpt a new one. This
brings us to Botox, the snicker-worthy subject at the heart of this
paper. In Botox use, optional injections of Botulinum toxin tem-
porarily deaden the face, Emmanuel Levinas' primary site of living encounter. With Botox, living objects elect to become a little
less lively. Botox represents an important ethical gesture: a face-first
plunge for living objects to meet dead objects halfway, to locate and
enhance what is inert in the living, and extend toward inaccessible
deadness with necrophiliac love and compassion. "Botox ethics"
hints at how Object-Oriented Feminism might subtly shift object-
oriented terms. Resistance to being known twists into resistance to
alienation. Concern with qualities of things reconstitutes as concern for qualities of relations. And, speculation on the real becomes
performance of the real. Botox ethics experientially transforms empathy for dead counterparts into comingled sympathy. Setting aside
aesthetic allure, Botox ethics shoots up.[75]

This powerful argument (or parts of it) were already implicit
in an early attempt (from October 2008) by Ben Woodard to
think speculative realism in relation to the object and ethics.[76]

75 Bogost, "Object Oriented Feminism."
76 Ben Woodard, "The Phallicized Face: Towards an Objectifying Ethics or the (Real) Object of Science," https://naughtthought.wordpress.
   com/2008/10/27/the-phallicized-face-towards-an-objectifying-ethics-or-
   the-real-object-of-science/. In his abstract on feminist metaphysics mentioned above Paul Reid-Bowen confesses that "the irony and/or perversity

Woodard's assertion, and this should bring to mind Bryant's argument about feminist thought and the biological body, is that "the philosophical paradigm of speculative realism can serve to elucidate an ethics of the Real object." For Woodard, Levinas "sweeps the phallus under the rug of the face" and he suggests that "the object, as a form of immanence" must be "brought into psychoanalysis and opposed to the formal object, the object as concept." In a typically Schellingian account of slime dynamics, Woodard turns to Iain Hamilton's Grant's nature philosophy to argue that "post-Kantian philosophies predominantly ignore the inorganic focusing instead on the opposition of number and animal, epitomized in the contrast between Deleuze and Badiou." As Woodard understands it, "inorganicity as the self construction of matter, as an ontological protoplasm — the slime of being — provides the very possibility of all philosophy." Behar's face-first plunge for "living objects to meet dead objects halfway" obliquely references Karen Barad's work on "agential realism," the way bodies intra-act, dynamically and causally.[77] It also

of proposing this alliance [between objects and objectification], given the history and weight of feminist analyses of sexual objectification, is not lost on me. However, I contend that an Object Oriented Ontology does not run afoul of ethical, political and social feminist critiques of objectification." Graham Harman comments on this by reminding us that the objects of oop have "nothing to do with objectification. In fact, they are what resist all objectification. To objectify someone or something is to limit it, to reduce it [...] by contrast, object-oriented philosophy is by definition an anti-reductionist philosophy. It holds that all things must be taken on their own terms. The reason for complaints about 'objectification' is that a false split is made between people and maybe animals who cannot be objectified, and inanimate objects which can. My thesis, by contrast, is that even inanimate objects should not and cannot be objectified." See http://doctorzamalek2.wordpress.com/2010/01/22/levi-on-reid-bowen-on-feminism-and-ooo/.

77 See Karen Barad, "Queer Causation and the Ethics of Mattering," in *Queering the Non/Human,* eds. Noreen Giffney and Myra Hird (Aldershot: Ashgate, 2008), 311–38; and "Quantum Entanglements and Hauntological Relations of Inheritance: Dis/continuities, SpaceTime Enfoldings, and Justice-to-Come," *Derrida Today* 3, no. 2 (2010): 240–68. In my preface, "The Open," to Giffney and Hird's *Queering the Non/Human* (xix–xx), I made a fairly early reference to the potential enmeshments of speculative realism and queer theory: "If for Haraway and many of the authors collected here

calls to mind Reza Negarestani's opening up of "the moment of nucleation with nigredo" and the mathesis of decay and pu-trefaction.[78] The meeting between queer theory and speculative realism involves a mutual blackening, a "necrophilic intimacy," a meeting of necrotizing forces: "if the intelligibility of the world must thus imply a 'face to face' coupling of the soul with the body qua dead, then intelligibility is the epiphenomenon of a necrophilic intimacy, a problematic collusion with the rotting double which brings about the possibility of intelligibility with-in an inert cosmos."[79] Queer theory and speculative realism/ object-oriented ontology are not so much open to, as opened by each other, in what Bogost calls "carpentry, doing philosophy by making things."[80]

The rest of the papers on the OOF panel turned their atten-tion to the body. Anne Pollock's "Heart Feminism" asks what

the question has been 'if we have never been human, then where do we begin?' then answers have been forthcoming in other fields: Bruno Latour's Actor Network Theory has been at the forefront of technoscientific atten-tion to (if not queering as such) the non-human, Bill Brown's and Sherry Turkle's probing of things and 'evocative objects' has foregrounded our in-timacy with the objects we live with in generative ways, Graham Harman's speculative realism has inaugurated a philosophy turned toward objects and consistently urged us towards a humanitarian politics a uned to the objects themselves, while Quentin Meillassoux's non-correlationism argues that there can be no necessary relations between things in a vision of the world a er finitude, a world without humans."

78 Reza Negarestani, "The Corpse Bride: Thinking with *Nigredo*," *Collapse* IV (Falmouth: Urbanomic, 2008), 129–61.

79 Ibid., 134–35. See also his "Death as a Perversion: Openness and Germinal Death," http://www.ctheory.net/articles.aspx?id=396. In my preface "TwO (Theory without Organs)" to David V. Ruffolo's *Post-Queer Politics* (Farn-ham: Ashgate, 2009), x, I make a connection between post-queer politics and Negarestani's polytics: "We might, borrowing from Reza Negarestani in *Cyclonopedia: Complicity with Anonymous Materials* [Melbourne: Re.Press, 2008], call this a 'polytics' of anomalous or unnatural participation with the outside, a set of 'schizotrategies' for openness and insurgency."

80 Bogost, "Object Oriented Feminism." This kind of mutual blackening is what has motivated much of the recent Black Metal Theory which shares some important overlaps with speculative realist thought.

"starting from the heart might offer for feminism,"[81] Adam Za-
retsky began to formulate an Object-Oriented Bioethics (OOB)
and Frenchy Lunning, in a paper on the corset, reflected on the
"anamorphic entangled fields of the feminine and the fetish."
Ian Bogost's extemporized response is interesting since it takes
us back to where we began: "I had the expectation that today's
speakers would define 'object-oriented feminism.' That they
would pin it down, that they would domesticate it, if you want."
But OOF is as undomesticatable as queer theory or speculative
realism. It refuses to be pinned down, anatomized, given a precise shape. Instead, Bogost tells us "we saw a fascinating exploration around a theme. A tour of sorts, a kind of Heideggerian
pastoral stroll on which aspects of object-oriented ontology
were introduced to aspects of feminist theory." We might sup-
plement Bogost's observation by saying that aspects of feminist
theory were also introduced to aspects of object-oriented ontology in a mutual illumination. As he himself writes in response
to Pollock, "going into the body also means going outside of
it, like a Möbius strip or a Klein bottle." And this idea extends
beyond the biological body because, for Bogost, we have been
shown "the value of looking for" Meillassoux's "great outdoors"
inside as well as outside. Object-oriented feminism is, and again
this should remind us of Bryant and Barad, "a perturbation of

81 With the exception of Peter Gratton (see his course syllabus here: http://
    web.me.com/grattonpeter/2010_Speculative_Realism/Speculative_
    Realism.html), the philosophy of Jean-Luc Nancy has been largely absent
    from speculative realist discourse which is strange given his attention to
    the sense of all beings-in-the-world, from the human to the animal to the
    inorganic. The best place to start on Nancy and "heart feminism" however
    would be his essay "The Heart of Things" in *The Birth to Presence,* trans. Bri-
    an Holmes and others (Stanford: Stanford University Press, 1993), 167–88.
    Jacques Derrida has been equally neglected (frequently ugly debates about
    Derrida have flared up from time to time in the SR blogosphere in the past
    year) in both SR and OOO thinking despite some claims that his philoso-
    phy anticipates some central OOO concepts. Again, if one simply wanted to
    start with "heart feminism" you could look to Derrida's book *On Touching:
    Jean-Luc Nancy,* trans. Christine Irizarry (Stanford: California University
    Press, 2005), where he ruminates on Nancy's heart transplant, technicity,
    and sexual difference.

human and world." Like Butler's iterability, this agential realism or materialism, which brackets things-in-phenomena, allows for new articulations, new configurations, for what Luciana Parisi calls "affective relations," a community constituted through Barad's posthuman performativity.[82] Such an ethico-politics (and the queering of the normativities of both queer theory and speculative realism themselves) depends on what Agamben calls "the open," a process which does not follow some preconceived teleological program. There can be no program for what queer

82 Luciana Parisi, "The Nanoengineering of Desire," in Giffney and Hird, *Queering the Non/Human,* 283–310. Parisi's work is heavily influenced by the blackened Deleuzoguattarianism of Nick Land and her book *Abstract Sex: Philosophy, Bio-Technology and the Mutations of Desire* maps a complex web of intricate relations between humans and non/humans. In an interview with Matthew Fuller she explains that: "Abstract Sex addresses human stratification on three levels. The biophysical, the biocultural and the bio-digital amalgamation of layers composing a constellation of bodies within bodies, each grappled within the previous and the next formation — a sort of positive feedback upon each other cutting across specific time scales. In other words, these levels of stratification constitute for *Abstract Sex* the endosymbiotic dynamics of organization of matter — a sort of antigenealogical process of becoming that suspends the teleology of evolution and the anthropocentrism of life. From this standpoint, the modalities of human optimism, rooted in the net substantial distinction between the good and the evil and the distinct belief in negative forces, fail to explain the continual collision and coexistence of the distinct layers. Following the law of morality, human optimism would never come to terms with its own paradoxes of construction and destruction. And if it does it is soon turned into an existential crisis giving in to the full force of negating power and thus all becomes intolerable. Once we are forced to engage with the way layers collide in the human species — the way some biophysical and biocultural sedimentations rub against each other under certain pressures and in their turn the way they are rubbed against by the biodigital mutations of sensory perception for example — then the moral stances of optimism and pessimism make no longer sense. Indeed we need to leap towards a plane debunked of ultimate moral judgement. A plane full of practice and contingent activities, where we nd ourselves plunged in a field of relation — interdependent ecologies of forces (a ractors, pressures, thresholds), which trigger in us modifications that resonate across all scales of organization." See http://www.nettime.org/Lists-Archives/nettime-l-0410/msg00054.html.

theory or speculative realism or object oriented approaches do. They are not means to an end but rather means "without end."[83]

Naught Thought: On Ben Woodard's Queer Speculative Realism

If for Bogost one of the promising aspects of OOF is that it looks for the great outdoors inside as well as outside, then we might not see Ben Woodard's nihilist speculative realism as an ally for object-oriented feminisms or queer theories. Indeed, in his most recent work Woodard has cautioned that philosophy can only ever return to the "great outdoors" if it "leaves behind the dead loop of the human skull."[84] That said, Woodard's essays on his *Naught Thought* blog have consistently led the way when it comes to queering speculative realism and to advancing the politics of a queered speculative realism. We have already seen his discussion of the "phallicization of ethics" but we might also consider his various writings on gender, sexuality, psychoanalysis, anorexia, and trauma as clearing a ground for queer speculations.[85] I will isolate just a few exemplary posts. As Bryant has reminded us, it is masculinism which forgets the real of the biological body and it is feminist thought which remembers it. One figure who has been largely forgotten by the speculative

---

83 Giorgio Agamben, *The Open: Man and Animal,* trans. Kevin Attell (Stanford: Stanford University Press, 2004) and *Means Without End: Notes on Politics,* trans. Vincenzo Binetti and Cesare Casarino (Minneapolis: University of Minnesota Press, 2000).

84 Ben Woodard, "Mad Speculation and Absolute Inhumanism: Lovecraft, Ligotti and the Weirding of Philosophy," *continent* 1, no. 1 (2011): 3–13, http://www.continentcontinent.cc/index.php/continent/article/view/14.

85 Woodard has engaged with the queer theories of Lauren Berlant on fetal citizenship, Ann Cvetkovich on affect, and Lee Edelman on reproductive futurism in a number of posts. For example see "Migrations of Trauma," http://naughtthought.wordpress.com/2008/01/19/migrations-of-trauma/ and "Trauma's Transmogrifications," http://naughtthought.wordpress.com/2007/10/27/traumas-transmogrifications/. Three other names one associates with speculative realism, Dominic Fox (who blogs at *Poetix*), Mark Fisher (who blogs at *K-Punk*), and Nina Power (who blogs at *Infinite Thought*), have also critiqued Edelman's book *No Future: Queer Theory and the Death Drive* (Durham: Duke University Press, 2004).

realists is Katerina Kolozova and Woodard returns her to her proper place in his post "Meshing the Real and the Transcendental or Katerina Kolozova."[86] He tells us that "jumping from Judith Butler, to Rosi Braidotti, to Drucilla Cornell, to Derrida, to Lacan (with thinkers such as Badiou, Derrida, and Deleuze sprinkled throughout) Kolozova formulates a breathtakingly lucid and powerfully political, theoretical and social system." One of the reasons why Kolozova has not been prominent in SR discussions is that speculative realism "has been more than slightly ambiguous as to its relation to psychoanalysis." Bryant and Negarestani are two very obvious counter-examples but Woodard cites Brassier's limp deployments of the term "unconscious" and its near absence in the texts of other speculative realists as evidence. But Kolozova's psychoanalytically inflected, Laruellian non-philosophical system, is clearly a prime, if again shunted to the margins, site for realist and non-correlationist thinking about the body, sexual difference, and identity:

> If, as Kolozova suggests, the body is the nearest bearer of the Real of our being, how do we articulate a politics which is different from the tired attempts of identity politics? If we carry the real with us, and our experiences can touch upon the real, what is to separate a politics of the embodied Real versus an identity politics? The difference that Kolozova ends on is that since identity is always a failure to grasp the Real and sense the World, as experiential, is what forces and faces the Real of such materialism, we can only remind ourselves that such a world is not-All, that the World can never grasp identity as such let alone any singular human in their automatic solitude. The strength here is that Kolozova seems bolder than Badiou in dismissing the pre-Evental non-subject and more optimistic than Transcendental Materialism in that not only can the subject think

---

86 Ben Woodard, "Meshing the Real and the Transcendental or Katerina Kolozova," http://naughtthought.wordpress.com/2008/06/24/meshing-the-real-and-the-transcendental-or-katerina-kolozova/.

the gap that it is but that the gap does the thinking, that the Real itself desires to be transcendental to, in a sense, be political.[87]

Shortly before this post on Kolozova's politics, Woodard had worked though a provisional speculative realist politics (in June 2008, two years exactly before Vitale's post on the lack of political engagement of sr), wisely rejecting Lee Edelman's *No Future* and its misleading politics of the Real along the way.[88] Woodard gently argues that the "End of Time" section of Brassier's *Nihil Unbound* "leans towards what might be a politics, in that, jumping from Freud's theory of the drive as repetition, there is an inherent will-to-know in humans that is, contrary to most of the universe, negentropic." The question he proceeds to ask is: "how does one account for the genesis of the multitude in a non-vitalist way, in a philosophically realist way, that does not occlude the possibility of politics?" He partially answers that speculative realism "provides a step in the right direction in that it illustrates the radicality of thought by 'immanentizing' the transcendental by binding it to the object." But the full answer he moves towards is that

> the implicit politics in Speculative Realism is found in its return to slime as the trace of life, that the smudge of materiality cannot be idealized away, not even in the most basic form of relation itself, in the notion of currency and exchange. This zero point of being is, in a sense, a paradoxically deanthropomorphized bio-politics — that matter matters in that it can think itself as such without recourse to the reflective structures of ethics or democracy. Speculative Realism exposes that the zombic hunger of Hardt and Negri's multitude is a form of thinking and not a form of being. The psychoanalytic contribution here is that capital, while inhabiting the drive's mode

87 Ibid.
88 Ben Woodard, "Heaps of Slime or Towards a Speculative Realist Politics," http://naughtthought.wordpress.com/2008/06/20/heaps-of-slime-or-towards-a-speculative-realist-politics/. In their interviews with Woodard in *The Speculative Turn* both Žižek and Badiou argue that speculative realism lacks political purchase.

of iteration, is still subject to alteration. In thinking capital as object we highlight the objects around it as possibly dissociable from it such as democracy and the social.

Conclusion: Some Sightings and Speculations

In *Circus Philosophicus*, Graham Harman asks us to imagine a "giant ferris wheel" with thousands "of separate cars, each of them loaded with various objects."[89] This final section paints a picture of several ferris wheels, each one containing glimpses of encounters between queer theory and speculative thought, which readers can then pause and fix in their minds as they continue to wheel around.

Ferris Wheel #1: Neomaterialist Feminism

This wheel would contain texts by various thinkers associated with (a mostly Deleuzian) neomaterialist or neovitalist feminism which has been sensitive to the nonhuman, the inorganic and the vibrancy of matter. This would include theorists such as Stengers,[90] Elizabeth Grosz,[91] Rosi Braidotti,[92] Manuel de Landa,[93] Myra Hird,[94] and Claire Colebrook.[95] It would also hold Jane Bennett's *Vibrant Matter: A Political Ecology of*

89 Harman, *Circus Philosophicus*, 1.
90 Isabelle Stengers, *Cosmopolitics* 1, trans. Robert Bononno (Minneapolis: University of Minnesota Press, 2010).
91 Elizabeth Grosz, *Chaos, Territory, Art: Deleuze and the Framing of the Earth* (New York: Columbia University Press, 2008).
92 Rosi Braidotti, *Transpositions: On Nomadic Ethics* (Cambridge: Polity, 2006).
93 Manuel DeLanda, *Philosophy and Simulation: The Emergence of Synthetic Reason* (London: Continuum, 2011). For a queering of DeLanda's work, see Jeff Lord's review of *A Thousand Years of Non-Linear History* here: http://www.situation.ru/app/j_art_1036.htm
94 Myra Hird, *Sex, Gender and Science* (Basingstoke: Palgrave, 2004). Hird is heavily influenced by Harman's work. Her recent issue of *Parallax* (16, no. 1, 2010) on the life of the gift contains Harman's essay "Asymmetrical Causation: Influence without Recompense."
95 Claire Colebrook, "How Queer Can You Go? Theory, Normality and Normativity," in Giffney and Hird, *Queering the Non/Human*, 17–34. Cole-

Things which rethinks the partition of the sensible (in Rancière's terms), where matter is seen as inert and human beings are understood as vibrant. She turns the "figures of 'life' and 'matter' around and around, worrying them until they start to seem strange [...] [and] in the space created by this estrangement, a *vital materiality* [of thunder storms, stem cells, fish oils, metal, trash, electricity] can start to take shape."[96]

Ferris Wheel #2: The Sex Appeal of the Inorganic
This wheel takes its name from Mario Perniola's book *Sex Appeal of the Inorganic* which strangely hasn't exerted much of an influence on speculative realism.[97] In it we would discover figures and texts desiring a re-cycling of the world, a world re-encountered in which each singular being is exposed to an existence they share with other beings (from shells, to hammers, to clouds, to crystals, to storms). The wonder involved in this encounter which shakes all our anthropocentric certainties, is we might say, after Sara Ahmed, a "queer phenomenology.'" In Ahmed's terms, a reorientation toward the world and its objects (tables and pebbles are among her gorgeous examples), such a making strange, is what "allows the familiar to dance with life again."[98] Among the other texts housed here would be those which return an agential dynamism to the non-living, the inanimate and the inert: Bernard Stiegler's *Technics and Time* which queers the distinction between man and animal by mining the paradox between the human invention of the technical

brook's emerging work on extinction might be useful for those thinking about politics and nature after Brassier and Woodard.

96 Jane Bennett, *Vibrant Matter: A Political Ecology of Things* (Durham and London: Duke University Press, 2010), vii. Jonathan Goldberg's recent thinking around Lucretian physics is pertinent here too. See, for one example, *The Seeds of Things: Theorizing Sexuality and Materiality in Renaissance Representations* (New York: Fordham University Press, 2009).

97 Mario Perniola, *Sex Appeal of the Inorganic* (London: Continuum, 2004).

98 Sara Ahmed, *Queer Orientations: Orientations, Objects, Others* (Durham and London: Duke University Press, 2006), 164. Ahmed has been highly critical of the masculinism of OOO.

and the technical invention of the human;[99] Nikki Sullivan and
Sam Murray's *Somatechnics* which plasticizes, intertwines and
enfolds man and animal, human and object;[100] Jeffrey Jerome
Cohen's "Stories of Stone," a geochoreographesis in which he
explores the life of stone, allowing it to breathe and speak as it
"confounds the boundary between organic and inorganic, art
and nature, human and mineral."[101] It would also include Shannon Bell's *Fast Feminism,* a philo-porno-political machine in
which she fucks Stelarc's six-legged walking robot and tissue-
engineers a male phallus, a female phallus, and a Bataillean big
toe in a "bioreactor where they formed into a neo-organ."[102] Also
here we would discover Dinesh Wadiwel's essay "Sex and the
Lubricative Ethic" where in the fisting scene a whole range of
"nonhuman material objects are also important entities within networks of erotic production. A sling, a piece of lingerie, a

99 Bernard Stiegler, *Technics and Time, 1: The Fault of Epimetheus,* trans. Rich-
    ard Beardsworth and George Collins (Stanford: Stanford University Press,
    2008).
100 Nikki Sullivan and Sam Murray (eds.), Somatechnics: *Queering the Tech-
    nologisation of Bodies* (Farnham: Ashgate Press, 2009). In my preface to the
    book, "Originary Somatechnicity," I wrote that they "disclose that there is
    not just an originary technicity but also an originary somaticisation of the
    technical object. Their queer intervention, the space they open for us in a
    deft disoriginating move, is to begin to think an origina somatechnicity"
    (xiii).
101 Jeffrey Jerome Cohen, "Stories of Stone," *postmedieval: a journal of medieval
    cultural studie*s 1, nos. 1/2 (2010): 56–63. Medieval Studies has proved to be
    a particularly fertile site for speculative realist thinking. Two other essays in
    the inaugural issue of *postmedieval* by Michael Witmore ("We Have Never
    Not Been Inhuman") and Julian Yates ("It's (for) You; or, the Tele-t-r/opical
    Post-Human") engage with Meillassoux and Harman. In her response essay,
    the feminist N. Katherine Hayles picks up on this and also references both
    Harman and Bogost when she writes that "alien phenomenologists gather
    information about tools to understand them not as accessories to human
    culture but as subjects that perceive and act in the world" (Hayles, "Posthu-
    man Ambivalence," 266).
102 Shannon Bell, *Fast Feminism* (New York: Autonomedia, 2010), 183.

whip or a vibrator may all play significant if not indispensable roles in enabling an erotic scene to happen."[103]

Ferris Wheel #3: Persons and Things
This wheel gets its name from Barbara Johnson's *Persons and Things* which isn't often remembered when speculative realists and object-oriented ontologists are reconfiguring relations between subjects and objects.[104] Bracha Ettinger's post-Lacanian work on the matrixial belongs here too.[105] It shares much on the level of style with Negarestani's psychoanalytic territopic materialisms;[106] her matrixiality may have affinities with Iain Hamilton Grant's dark chemistry of ur-slime;[107] and she makes it clear how Meillassoux's hyperchaos also refers to the absolute contingency of gender.

Ferris Wheel #4: Object-Oriented Maternity
Ettinger could also take her place in this wheel alongside Lisa Baraitser's *Maternal Encounters* where she theorizes maternal "stuff," the many objects which encumber the mother's body. These "maternal objects" are variously figured by Baraitser as Latourian "actants" or Harmanian "tool-beings." And these tool-beings include clothes, blankets, quilts, bottles, teats, milk powder, sterilizers, breast pumps, feeding spoons and bowls, juice bottles and bibs, pacifiers, mobiles, rattles, nappies, wipes, changing mats, creams, powders, cribs, cots, baskets, baby mon-

---

103 Dinesh Wadiwel, "Sex and the Lubricative Ethic," in *The Ashgate Research Companion to Queer Theory,* eds. Noreen Giffney and Michael O'Rourke (Farnham: Ashgate Press, 2009), 492.
104 Barbara Johnson, *Persons and Things* (Cambridge: Harvard University Press, 2008).
105 Bracha Lichtenberg Ettinger, *The Matrixial Borderspace* (Minneapolis: University of Minnesota Press, 2006).
106 Reza Negarestani, "On the Revolutionary Earth: A Dialectic in Territopic Materialism," http://fass.kingston.ac.uk/downloads/conference-dark-materialism-paper.pdf.
107 Iain Hamilton Grant, "Being and Slime: The Mathematics of Protoplasm in Lorenz Oken's 'Physio-Philosophy,'" *Collapse IV* (Falmouth: Urbanomic, 2008), 287–321.

itors, mobiles, prams, buggies, carry cots, slings, back packs, car seats and so ever infinitely on.[108]

Ferris Wheel #5: Here Comes Everything!
The ferris wheels of speculative realism, object-oriented ontology, and queer theory have been shown to be interlocking or each perhaps as tiny wheels imagined inside each other. If Bryant hopes that speculative realism and OOO will create projects for others, then what we need to ensure is that the wheels keep spinning and that we never try to pin things down. If we refuse to spell out a programmatic content for speculative thought, then it will always retain the power to wrench frames and whenever and wherever queer theory (or better queer theories) and speculative realism (or better speculative realisms) meet, that "fantastic explosion"[109] promises an irreducible openness to everything.

108 Lisa Baraitser, *Maternal Encounters: The Ethics of Interruption* (London: Routledge, 2009), 126.
109 Timothy Morton, "Queer Ecology," 273.

Printed in Great Britain
by Amazon